Panorama
of
The Villages

Annette Mach

Photograph Credits

Bancroft Library, University of California Berkeley
Cole, Lucie - Feral boars
Cribari, Albert - Cribari Family
Frasse, Ebe Cribari - Cribari Family
Hinrichs, Scott - The Villages
Hughes, Ed, East Bay Regional Park District - Ohlone
Kulakofsky, Michael - Villages' Birds
Mach, Annette - The Villages
Mach, Richard - The Villages
Martin Luther King Library - Maps
Oregon State University Archives - Prune Orchards
Ortiz, Marcos - Villages web site art
San José History Museum - Evergreen
San Jose State University Archaeological Department
Smith, Jerry - Albert Haentze Collection
Stednitz, Betty - The Villages
Tearse, Claire - Bisceglia Family Collection
The Villages Golf and Country Club - The Villages, Wehner
"The Villager", The Villages Golf and Country Club
Williamson, Sandra, GeoCadd Surveys - aerial photograph
Wines and Vines Magazine - Winery History

© 2010 Annette Mach
© 2010 Cover design Richard and Annette Mach
ISBN 978-1-4507-3793-7

Printed in the United States of America
PrintPenquin
48503 Milmont Drive - Fremont, CA 94538
2010

This book is dedicated to

my husband, Richard

and

my daughters, Cathryn, Laura, Diana

for all their advice and loving support.

Contents

Preface

1. Ohlone Indians   1

2. Rancho Yerba Buena and the City of San José   8

3. John McCarty   14

4. Our Early Neighbors   15

5. William Gottlieb Wehner   29

6. Albert Haentze   37

7. The Mirassou Family   42

8. The Cribari Family   47

9. The Villages Golf and Country Club   57

10. The Twelve Villages   125

11. Clubs and Organizations   139

12. Volunteers and Gifts   149

13. The Villager   157

14. Geology and Earthquakes   161

15. Fauna and Flora   166

16. Epilogue   182

17. Bibliography   183

Preface

When I began this journey of recording the history of The Villages, I had no idea where it would lead me. It has opened doors that I never realized existed. My intent was to give a full picture of the land and the people who inhabited it from the days of the Ohlone Indians, the Spanish Rancho, the vineyards and eventually to the present day of life as we know it.

Many have asked me why I was doing this project. My answer is, "I love The Villages, the total environment and especially the people." This area that we live in is so rich in history and I feel very strongly that; history not recorded is history lost.

As I made this journey, I was very fortunate to meet and talk with many descendants of the families who lived on this land prior to the development of The Villages. The help and information that they shared was invaluable.

Along the way, many people have supported me in this endeavor and my heart-felt thanks go to each of them. First and foremost is my husband, Dick who listened tirelessly to my excitement and frustrations as well as proofing the many drafts of this book. Mary Tatum and Julia Meadows gave me the acceptance of my proposal, as well as encouragement along the way. They dug out papers and photographs from the archives and answered my never-ending questions. Darren Shaw gave me continued encouragement as well as some proof reading. Chuck Elderton, with his love of history, gathered photographs and assisted with the proofing,

Another door opened when I met Alan Leventhal, an archeologist from San José State University who shared his research of the Ohlone Indians. Not to be forgotten are the many Villagers who supplied information for specific areas of the book.

My wish is that as you read this, you also, will become entrenched in the history of this place that we call home.

Annette

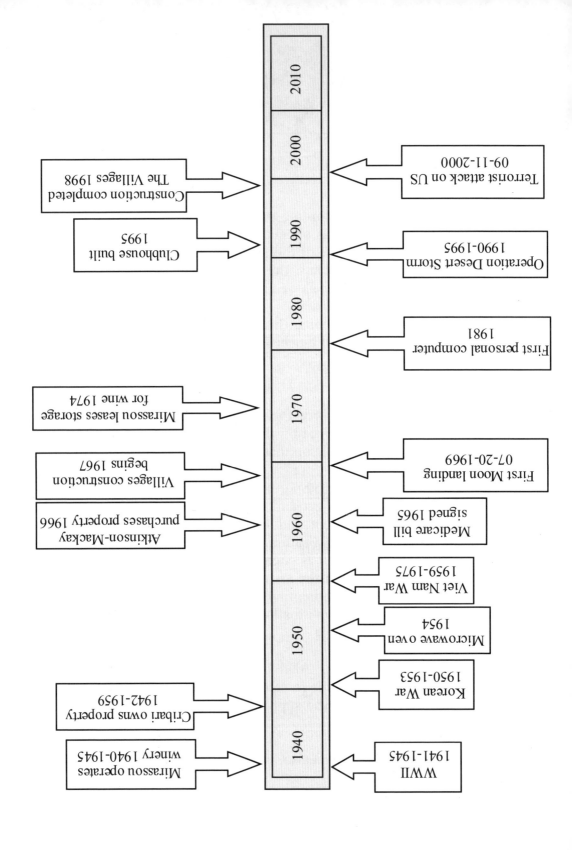

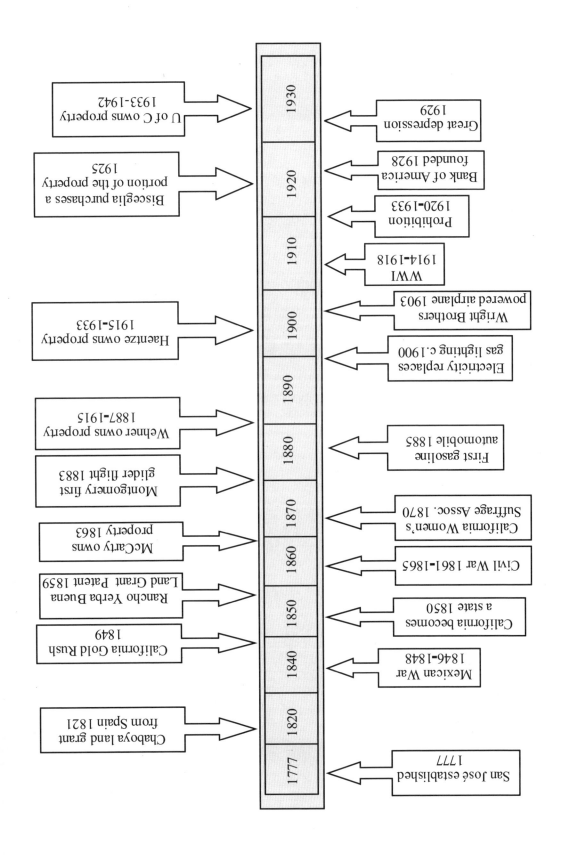

Ohlone Indians

The land was fertile and ablaze with oak trees, berries, wildflowers and plentiful water. Animals abounded. Deer, elk, antelope, rabbits, foxes, mountain lions, black bears and grizzly bears roamed the hills and valleys. Steelhead trout, salmon and other fish were found in the larger creeks, streams and in the bay.

Stories told to ship captains that were recorded in meticulous, detailed notes in their journals of the early trading vessels and the missionary's writings gave us much of the knowledge about these early people who dwelled on the land that was to become Rancho Yerba Buena. Archaeologists and anthropologists did extensive study in this area around 1900. A few semi-permanent settlements in the Santa Clara Valley date back to at least A.D. 500. There is also some evidence that the Ohlones migrated from the Sacramento area by way of the Sacramento River, ultimately settling in the Santa Clara Valley.

"They believe that their tribes originally came from the north", said Captain Frederick Beechey (an English naval officer and geographer). The Ohlones knew little of their own history. They were forbidden to talk of the dead, speak their names or tell of their deeds.

The Ohlone Indians were the earliest inhabitants of the San Francisco Bay area, extending from San Francisco to Big Sur, south of Monterey. Before the Spaniards arrived, Central California had the densest Indian population in California, north of Mexico. It is estimated approximately 30,000 Costanoan/Ohlones lived in this area.

The Ohlones were not a tribe such as Sioux, Hopi or Navajo. There were about forty tribal groups who each had their own territory and customs. Not much is known about the Ohlones specifically. Most of the information gathered by sea captains and missionaries was based on the customs of the nearby tribes of the Yokuts and the Miwoks. There is some thought that *Ohlone* might have also been the name of a Tribal group (Oljon) along the Pacific Coast.

From what we know, they were very much engaged in warfare, and cared for the land upon which they settled. There appear to have been villages that were on the eastern shores of San Francisco Bay on high ground, close to fresh water creeks that supplied their needs. Their life was ordered and in tune with nature and the will of the creator. The mountain lions and grizzly bears that roamed through the mountains were the primary threat to their lives.

Courtesy of the Bancroft Library

The Ohlones followed the ancient patterns of fishing, hunting and gathering. In addition to the acorns and wild animals, they gathered berries, seeds, roots, shellfish and hunted other small animals such as rabbits, squirrels and birds. Insects, grasshoppers, lizards, snakes, moles, mice, gophers, wood rats, quail, doves and song birds were also part of their diet. Eagles, buzzards, ravens, owls and frogs were taboo for religious reasons.

When the Spanish and Anglo settlers arrived in the late 1700's, they were quite disturbed with the eating habits of the Ohlones. To the settlers, gorging was a sin. They did not understand that the Ohlones ate what was plentiful at the time, according to the harvest. One missionary noted in his journal, "It is futile to exhort them to moderation; for their principle is 'If there is much to eat, let us eat much.' "

By their own standards, the Spanish settlers also found the Ohlone lazy. The Ohlone would work tirelessly during times when the salmon were running and during the seed and acorn harvest. In-between, there was little to do and the Ohlone would relax and play. Again, the Europeans were disturbed by these practices as they considered laziness a sin and hard work was a God given condition of human life.

Courtesy of San José State University Archeology Department

Courtesy of San José State University Archeology Department

In 1964, a team of archaeologists from San José State College, led by Professor Dean Pritchett conducted an excavation on Blauer Ranch; now The Villages. Artifacts such as small tools were found, as well as two skeletons. The first was of a young girl of about 16 and the second

of an older man about 27 years of age. They were removed carefully and transported to the Stanford Museum. When archaeologist Michael Fong of Basin Research Associates was examining the skeletons, he discovered that most of the Ohlones suffered from arthritis. He said, "This meant that they led vigorous lives."

In 2010, a second team from San José State University, led by Professor Alan Leventhal returned to the site in order to verify the location. This site is now identified as the Blauer Ranch site. The sitings done at that time places the archeological dig someplace between Sur Verano and the 5th tee on the golf course. Carbon dating on the skeletons was also done and it was determined that the burial date of these Indians was AD 345 (1665 years ago). The Roman Emperor, Constantine was in power.

Courtesy of The San Jose Mayfair

Inside their homes were blankets of deer and rabbit skins. Hamper baskets would be overflowing with seeds and roots the Ohlones had gathered, as well as dried meat and fish. Stored overhead in the rafters would be the supplies for basket making and tools such as awls, bone scrapers, file stones, obsidian knives and drills for making holes in beads. Obsidian is a natural volcanic glass formed into igneous rock. Due to its characteristics, the obsidian, along with flint was also used for arrow heads. Also stored in the rafters were their other hunting tools; fish traps, snares and ducks. The ducks were stuffed with tule grasses (tule grasses are large bulrushes found by wet lands in California) which were used as duck decoys.

The Ohlones had multiple permanent to semi-permanent villages within their territory that was approximately 100 square miles. Each triblet had a major village site, but they were routinely on the move as they followed the harvest. The elderly and the infirmed would remain behind at the village while the rest of the family traveled. Frequently, a member of the family would return to visit in order to be certain those left behind were fed and comfortable.

Ohlone Winter Camp, an artistic rendering, Hylkema, 1988

Courtesy of the East Bay Regional Park District

Because of their wandering lifestyle, permanent wooden style structures for their homes were non-existent. They lived in dome-shaped tule huts. The tule huts were very efficient. The dome shape helped to retain warmth and was relatively easy to construct. The tule however, tended to rot quickly, but since they moved so frequently, this was not a major concern. This was another practice of the ways of the Ohlones that the Europeans struggled to understand, because they valued permanence in their homes.

The huts were built on a framework of bent willow poles and then covered with the tule rush. In addition to these, there were also storage huts. The latter were built up on stilts to prevent them from being flooded during the winter rains. Acorns were stored in these huts for drying.

There were a proliferation of Coast Live Oak trees at that time in the Evergreen Valley (hence the name Evergreen), which was a source of food for the Ohlones. They would gather the acorns from the trees and store them in the huts for future use. They would hull the acorns, then dry and grind them into powder. The powder was leached by boiling to remove the bitter tannic acid. The moistened powder was then roasted and made into mush or bread.

The chief's residence was larger as he had the responsibility of entertaining guests from other areas. He also had more baskets filled with food for entertaining.

After the winter rains, the tule huts would become soggy and the land, marshy. The trails would become too muddy for walking long distances. The hills became a lush, velvety green, but unlike today, this green would last throughout much of the summer.

Huge mounds of seashells and ashes mixed with the soil were their mortuaries for nobility. In the early 1900's hundreds of these mounds could still be seen.

Instead of dugouts and plank boats, the Ohlones built their boats out of tule rushes, which generally only lasted for one season.

Courtesy of the East Bay Regional Park District

Men and women were shoeless. The women wore skirts of tule reeds and deer-skins. They decorated their faces with tattoos drawn in patterns of lines and dots. Adorning their necks were elaborate necklaces which they had created from the abundant supply of feathers and seashells, found along the shoreline.

Instead of pottery containers, the Ohlones preferred baskets for the simple reason of weight and the frequency of moving from place to place carrying their supplies.

Many of the men in the village would have two wives while the chief would have three. Different villages within the Ohlone tribe spoke different languages.

Ohlone Dancers at Mission San José
(Rezanov/Langsdorff Expedition)
Courtesy of Muwekama Ohlone Tribe of the
San Francisco Bay Area

The Ohlones felt that "To be wealthy was not to have; to be wealthy was to give." Therefore they did not focus on wealth and possessions. In fact, after a person died, all their poss-essions were destroyed. The Spaniards, when they arrived, found this very disappointing. They expected to find art-ifacts such as what was found in the Aztec and Inca empires. From their per-spective, this was failure.

The Spaniards began to settle in this area in 1776. Missionary books reveal a story about Father Pedro Font and Juan Bautista de Anza coming upon an Indian on March 31, 1776, who acted very fearful. They wrote that they didn't believe the Indian had ever seen Spaniards prior to this time.

When the missionaries arrived, their plan was to create the perfect community. The Ohlones would be part of the community for about ten years (from about 1769-1823) during which they would serve an apprenticeship. After these ten years, they would be given land of their own. The Franciscan Fathers set up ten missions on the Ohlone land between 1770 and 1797. The missions filled quickly until there were about 10,000 Ohlone at each mission.

In 1806, a measles epidemic claimed over 300 lives at Mission Dolores in San Francisco and only 23 infants were born alive. Later, thousands died in a ten year smallpox epidemic at Mission San José alone. By 1834, the Ohlone life and their crafts were becoming neglected and/or lost.

In the late 1820's, Mexico won its independence from Spain. In 1834, the new government ordered the California missions and their lands be turned over to the government. The Indians no longer had their homes or work. They had become accustomed to the structure and protection of mission life. Their new freedom was deemed by many to be a disaster. Some of them found work at nearby farms and ranches. Others formed small bands and took to hunting animals which gave them the name of outlaws. Many of the remaining Ohlones banded together in small ghetto-like communities. Slowly, bits and pieces of their old life style returned. This continued until the late nineteenth century. Records indicate the last structure was torn down in 1900. By 1935, the last full-blooded Ohlone died.

Traces of these settlements were found by archeologists when they were conducting environmental impact studies for The Meadowlands and The Silver Creek Valley Country Club. They found arrow heads, scrapers, knives, mortars and pestles, dart heads, and grinding stones. It wasn't until 1972, when a California State law was passed requiring that construction stop when human remains are found.

There are still descendents of the Ohlone Indians, living in the San Francisco and Monterey Bay area who comprise the present-day Muwekma Ohlone Tribe of the San Francisco Bay area (representing Missions Santa Clara, San José and Dolores); the Amah-Mutsum Tribal Band (representing Mission San Juan Buatista) and Esselen Nation (representing Missions San Carlos, Carmel and Soledad).

Rancho Yerba Buena and the City of San José

San José, California, the city that would eventually encompass The Villages, was established on November 29, 1777 as El Pueblo de San José de Guadalupe. The settlement was established upon the recommendation of Don Felipe de Neve, Governor of California under King Carlos III of Spain. This was one year after the United States had declared their independence from England.

San José's development was phenomenal – from a small farming community to the heart of today's Silicon Valley. The fruit tree orchards that gave San José the name of The Valley of Hearts Delight were gradually replaced by homes and industry.

In San José's early years, grain and livestock were the main products, then olives and grapes and other fruit trees. The year 1824 saw the mining of quicksilver (mercury, as we know it) in New Almaden, with the processing plant near what is now Silver Creek. Quicksilver was a vital component in the extraction of gold from the rock.

California's journey from a territory to ultimate statehood was long and fraught with conflict. For the first quarter of the nineteenth century, California was under the rule of King Carlos III of Spain and as a result it became part of the Mexican Republic on March 25, 1825.

Looking toward statehood, from April 1846 to February 1848, California was engaged in a war for independence from Mexico. After many battles, on June

14, 1846 in the California town of Sonoma, the Mexican General Vallejo was forced to surrender to what was referred to as a Band of Americans. After the surrender, the Americans took a piece of white fabric and painted a gold star and a grizzly bear on it. They added the words California Republic and rose what was to become the new state flag. This battle was known as The Bear Flag Revolt. Conflict continued between the Mexicans and the Americans, until the Treaty of Guadalupe–Hidalgo was signed in 1848 that ended the Mexican War.

This was followed by the writing of a state constitution in September 1849. San José was designated the first capital of California. This was not to be permanent and the capital made several moves until it was ultimately located in its present location, Sacramento.

September 9, 1850, California was given statehood and became the 31st state in the United States. Peter Hardeman Burnett was the first governor of California. Millard Fillmore was President at the time, assuming the office after the death of Zachery Taylor.

The community of Evergreen, founded in the late 1800's, was situated on Rancho Yerba Buena, about six miles southeast of San José. El Pueblo de San José de Guadalupe and Rancho Yerba Buena were located in the Santa Clara Valley bordered on the west by the coastal range of the Santa Cruz Mountains, beyond which is the Pacific Ocean and on the east by the Diablo Range.

Towering above the area at a height of 4,200 feet is the majestic Mount Hamilton, home to some spectacular scenery, wildflowers and Lick Observatory. Mount Hamilton was named after Laurentine Hamilton, a Presbyterian minister who arrived in California in 1855. He built and served a church in Columbia, California in the gold country. Shortly after, he moved to San José and served as the minister at the first Presbyterian Church of San José. In 1861, Mr. Hamilton hiked to the top of what was to become Mount Hamilton with his friend, William Brewer, who was the head of the California Geological survey. Mr.

Brewer named the mountain after his friend Hamilton.

Atop the mountain today is the white, dome shaped Lick Observatory that can be seen for miles around. In addition to several telescopes, the observatory boasts a refractor telescope on a moveable pedestal, still used by astronomers.

James Lick

The observatory was named after James Lick. Mr. Lick was born in Pennsylvania and as a young man moved to South America, where he established himself as a piano builder. One of his neighbors there was Domingo Ghirardelli who made chocolate. In 1848, Lick departed for San Francisco, bringing with him his tools and 600 pounds of cocoa beans. He arrived just days before the discovery of gold at Sutter's Mill. He was drawn to gold mining and along with many others had little success. He returned to San Francisco, invested in property and sold chocolate. This was a prosperous time in San Francisco due to the gold rush, and as a result, Lick became very wealthy.

Ghirardelli followed in 1849, settling in Stockton after also having failed at gold prospecting. Lick was very successful selling the chocolate in San Francisco and convinced his friend, Ghirardelli to join him. This was the birth of Ghirardelli Chocolate in San Francisco.

Lick moved south to the then sparsely populated Santa Clara Valley. He established a flour mill on the Guadalupe River in Santa Clara near the town of San José. Next to the mill, he built a granary and a twenty-seven room mansion that are still standing and are recognized as historic landmarks. (The mansion is at 554 Mansion Park Drive.)

Lick's next venture was a large garden project called Lick's Gardens in San José. He had trees and shrubs imported from around the world. To aid in his horticultural development, Lick ordered a large glass conservatory from an East Coast company. After a local newspaper ridiculed him in print, (he was considered an eccentric) he left the conservatory in its crates. Following his death in 1876, the conservatory was erected in Golden Gate Park in San Francisco. Lick had accumulated a fortune over his lifetime and generously donated hundreds of thousands of dollars to various beneficiaries; one of which helped to build the Lick Observatory on Mount Hamilton.

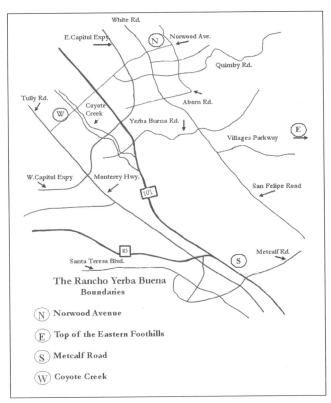

Rancho Yerba Buena y Socayre was the official name of the land granted to Don Antonio Chabolla by King Carlos (Charles) III of Spain in 1821 and confirmed by The United States Courts. Yerba Buena means Good Grass and *Socayre* is an unidentified Indian word. The Rancho covered the territory bounded by Coyote Creek, the Evergreen Hills and the present Norwood Avenue and Metcalf Road. Governor Figueroa (Governor of Alta California) granted the 24,342.64 acres to Don Antonio Chabolla in 1833 and the United States issued a patent for this land in 1859.

It is now known as the Evergreen section of San José.

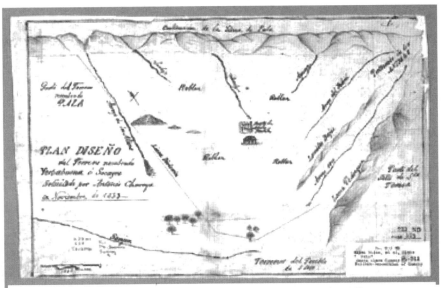

Rancho Yerba Buena 1833 Courtesy Martin Luther King Library

Abraham Lincoln was President of the United States at the time and he passed homestead legislation that would later affect the land grants in California. The Homestead Act stated, in part that an applicant could be given title to up to 160 acres of undeveloped federal land outside of the original thirteen colonies.

The law required three steps: file an application, improve the land and file for deed title. In addition an applicant must be 21 years of age or the head of the family, a United States citizen and must have never taken up arms against the U.S. Government.

Don Antonio Chabolla (hereafter known as Chaboya) was born in 1805 in Catalonia, Spain. He was the first Spanish settler in the Evergreen Valley when he moved there about 1820.

In early 1861, forty years after being granted the land and the same year that the Civil War began, there was a Settlers War on Antonio Chaboya's rancho. A large group of Americans settled on his Rancho, believing it to be public domain. They were given a "writ of ejectment" when the United States confirmed it belonged to Chaboya. The settlers refused to leave and enlisted the help of neighbors. Sheriff John Murphy summoned a posse to oust the settlers and assigned his group a meeting place. Although the men arrived for the posse at the appointed hour, they refused to go with the sheriff and were subsequently dismissed.

A Milpitas farmer by the name of Alfred Doten, (one of the men of the posse) gathered some friends on his own and according to his diary, they "rode out to the seat of the war". They found 2,000 settlers all armed…"two cannons, several flags, etc." At 1:00 p.m. Doten and his friends started for town along with the settlers. "There were eighty-three carriages, some with ladies, a band and about 1,000 horsemen with rifles and shotguns." They rode to Washington Square, which is now the location of the San José State University Campus. Sheriff Murphy spoke to them. The crowd cheered Murphy and "gave three groans for the land sharks and three more for the lawyer Matthews" and then dispersed peaceably. Chaboya had hired Jessie B. Hart and William Matthews to secure the United States patent for his grant. He paid the lawyers' fees in land instead of cash.

Subsequently, Antonio Chaboya sold off his land in smaller parcels to ranchers that came to the area. One of the parcels was a cemetery which Chaboya gave to the city of San José in 1839. Today the cemetery is known as Oak Hill Cemetery (on Curtner Road in San José) which has the distinction of being the oldest public cemetery in California.

Jesse B. Hart, one of the lawyers, later sold his parcel of land to Henry Pierce who was originally a New York native. Pierce came across the country to Santa Cruz in 1850, the same year that California became a state. He joined the throngs of people looking for gold. After his arrival, he married Martha Leibbrandt and they built a home on what is the Kuhn Ranch in Evergreen. This property is located on the Old Yerba Buena Road that winds up into the hills behind The Villages.

The road that runs east and west in front of The Villages' entrance, San Felipe Road was actually named for a small settlement in a valley ten miles east of Gilroy. In 1876 they had a post office, general store, tobacco farm and a factory for making cigars. The settlement is now totally erased.

A significant piece of history took place in 1860. Galloping across the country from St. Joseph, Missouri to San Francisco, California was the Pony Express. Though it only existed until October 1861, (a mere eighteen months), it is an event that has intrigued adults and children alike. It served to open an avenue of communication to and from the west coast. That same year, the transcontinental telegraph line was born. It was completed in October, 1861, putting the Pony Express out of business. The last letters by the Pony Express were delivered in November that same year.

By 1869 the Transcontinental Railroad opened between the Atlantic and Pacific coasts. It is considered one of the greatest American technological feats of the 19th century. The benefits of the railroad are well-known, but particularly so for the wine business in California. As the wine industry developed, the need for shipping became of utmost importance.

John McCarty

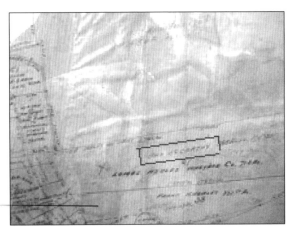

Map courtesy of the Martin Luther King Library

One of the ranchers that purchased a part of the Yerba Buena land grant was John McCarty who emigrated from County Cork, Ireland in 1849 at the age of 21. Mc Carty settled in Lynn, Massachusetts for his first five years in this country before traveling to California via Nicaragua. Interestingly, the course through Nicaragua at one time was considered as a possible location for a canal.

For the next five years, he moved from place to place, seeking employment. One year he worked in a sawmill at Bolinas in Marin County; then left to peddle fruit to residents in Grass Valley and Nevada City. Just 12 months later, he sold this business and found employment in the hoisting works of the Allison Ranch mine. From there he hopped between San Francisco, Benicia, and Suisun in Solano County, Sacramento, Marysville, Wyandotte, Springtown, Mountain Spring and back to Sacramento.

In September 1859, he traveled back to the East Coast, returning to Grass Valley, California the following year. Further moves within California took him to Napa and then to San José in Santa Clara County where he fits into this history.

After being in San José for one year, in 1863, he married Mary Gaveney and purchased part of the Yerba Buena land grant in Evergreen. The parcel that he purchased was comprised of 718 acres of land that was divided into stock range and arable land. He ranched and farmed this land until 1887 when he sold the land to William Wehner.

Childless, John McCarty died in 1891 and his wife, Mary eight years later.

McCarty Ranch Drive in Village Olivas is named for John McCarty.

Our Early Neighbors

The property on which The Villages sits, as well as the surrounding area is rich in history. It was developed by early pioneers who worked the land as well as providing grass covered acreage for the grazing of cattle. Learning the sagas of these men and women gives us an appreciation of the land on which we walk, ride and live daily. One just has to look at the hillside and imagine horses and buggies, farm equipment, and women in long dresses ringing the bell for the men to come in for dinner.

One of the earliest settlers in Evergreen was John Hassler. He emigrated from Goppingen, Germany in 1852 at the age of 32, right at the height of the gold rush. He became a United States citizen in 1867. After arriving in this country, he worked for James Lick at his flour mills and for the Miller and Lux cattle ranch before purchasing his own piece of land.

Hassler purchased 662 acres of the Rancho Yerba Buena land grant from Antonio Chaboya in 1856 and ended up paying for his land three times to ensure his ownership. This land was south west of Yerba Buena and Silver Creek Roads and on the west side of San Felipe Road. Hassler raised livestock and farmed the land. He planted beautiful eucalyptus groves and built stone walls to keep his livestock from roaming. One of his biggest challenges was protecting his land from the prospectors and squatters.

Five of Hassler's siblings also immigrated and settled in Santa Clara County. He had three married sisters, one of whom died in childbirth. His two brothers, Gottlieb and Adam remained bachelors and also farmed 160 acres of the Rancho Yerba Buena. Their piece was along Aborn and Silver Creek Roads.

John Hassler married Ann Henderson in 1870 and had seven children. One of his sons, John Hassler II married Mineola Wheeler who served as matron of the Women's Relief Corps Home in Evergreen (story follows later in this chapter).

Mr. Hassler and a man named Cottle helped in the development of a school in 1866 that was located at the intersection of White and Aborn Roads. This school was attended by the children of the vintners, Haentze, Mirassou and Bisceglia who later developed the Rancho Yerba Buena property.

Courtesy of San José History Museum

The early developers of The Villages had good foresight naming many of the streets in The Villages after ranchers from adjoining lands. This enables modern day residents to have some appreciation of the heritage of the land on which they live.

Nick Gerdts settled on the Chaboya land grant in the Evergreen area. He emigrated from Germany in 1891 with his brother and sister, when he was 19 years old. The 450 acres that he rented from Chaboya is the land where the Eastridge shopping center is located today. By 1915, he had saved enough money to purchase 34 acres from Chaboya on San Felipe Road. This property was located just south of Villages Parkway. He plowed the fertile land and planted a vineyard as well as prune, apricot and walnut orchards. He and his wife, Gretchen had two sons.

One of his sons, Henry along with his wife also became ranchers. As a result of Henry's interest in farming and ranching, he became one of the founders of the local 4H Club. (In the late 1800's young people were beginning to leave the rural areas and move to the cities. By 1905, 4H groups were in every state with their purpose to "...educate the youth of the county, town and city to a knowledge of their dependence on nature's resources and to the value of the fullest development of hand, head and heart..."). Henry Gerdts also became very involved with the Santa Clara County Fair, starting in 1946. Maintaining his involvement, for many years he became well-known for his service to the fair. Gerdts Drive is a street in Village Montgomery.

 Another orchard along San Felipe Road was owned by Otis Butler Whaley. Whaley settled in Sunnyvale and developed an orchard after moving here from Illinois. Moving from Sunnyvale, he farmed land in Almaden that he leased, before moving to Evergreen. He and his wife, Martha had six sons. Whaley purchased a parcel of land on San Felipe Road in 1911 and named it Sunnyslope Farm. The orchard consisted of prunes and apricots. The housing development, The Meadowlands, bordering on the southern boundary of The Villages, is situated on this parcel of land. Whaley served on the Evergreen Board of Trustees for 27 years. The O. B. Whaley Elementary School in the Evergreen School District, located on Alvin Avenue was named for him. Mr. Whaley died in 1946 at the age of 75. Whaley Drive is another street in Village Montgomery.

George Blauer purchased his farm on San Felipe Road about 1910. He was a California native with a Swiss father. His property was primarily on the west side of San Felipe Road, although a small section flowed over to the east side where The Villages now stands. George and his wife Clara lived down the road from Hassler according to the 1910 census. He started out farming his piece of land and about 1930 was employed as the District Manager for California Lands, Inc. The Blauers had three daughters; Catherine and Elizabeth and Georgene. The archeological dig mentioned earlier was on a section of this land. Blauer Lane is right next to Whaley Drive in Village Montgomery.

Along with the ranch land, some of the parcels that Chaboya sold were for commercial uses. In the late 1800's, shops and services opened along San Felipe Road in order to provide ranchers and farmers with their needs and supplies. These shops eventually made up the small village of Evergreen.

One of the shops on the west side of San Felipe was Andy's Garage (owned by Andy Parola), built to service the farm and ranch equipment of the settlers. The garage still exists today as Hinman's Garage.

Courtesy San José History Museum

Across San Felipe Road from Andy's Garage was a General Merchandise store owned by Joe Smith. He opened it in about 1867 and was the proprietor for 58 years. This was the first General Merchandise store east of the city of San José.

Courtesy San José History Museum

In the same area was Kettman's Saloon. c.1870

Courtesy San José History Museum

Along with these commercial enterprises in the Village of Evergreen was Lyceum Hall, where many performances were held. It was located on the west side of San Felipe Road in the heart of the small village.

Henry W. Coe

If you have ever hiked up into the hills in back of The Villages you would see, (just beyond the fence), rolling, grass-covered hills. This piece of property was developed as a cattle ranch by Henry Willard Coe in 1870.

The fence that borders The Villages' property was originally a moss-covered wooden fence. Nancy Coe, Henry W. Coe's great-granddaughter said in an interview in 1991 that the redwood fencing was over one hundred years old. It had deteriorated and could no longer serve the purpose of confining the grazing cattle on the Coe Ranch as well as the cattle on The Villages' property. In 1995, 3,000 feet of the old fence were torn down and replaced with metal posts and barbed wire. In the process, the original square nails that had been used in the wooden fence were found.

After arriving here from the state of New Hampshire in 1847, Henry Coe settled in the Willows (now Willow Glen) area of San José. (Coe Avenue in Willow Glen is named for him.) Mr. Coe raised silk worms and he made the first silk American Flag. This flag is now housed in the Smithsonian Institution in Washington, D.C.

Mr. Coe developed the self-preserving process for drying fruit which was used by the farmers in the valley. He also raised hops which he exported to Germany. Hops are used to flavor and stabilize beer. Coe purchased 4,000 acres in East San José that extended as far as Morgan Hill. It is this piece of property that borders The Villages. He also had an additional 13,000 acres east of Coyote.

View of the Coe Ranch

Henry Coe had two sons, Charles Willard Coe and Henry Willard Coe, Jr. who inherited the property. After Charles married and moved to southern California, he released his portion to his brother Henry.

In the early 1900's, Henry Coe, Jr. married Rhoda Dawson Sutcliff and they homesteaded property near Morgan Hill and named it the Pine Ridge Ranch. They moved back to the Evergreen ranch in 1913, but retained the Morgan Hill parcel. They had two children, Henry Sutcliff Coe and Sada Sutcliff Coe. Henry Sutcliff Coe inherited the Pine Ridge property after his father's death. Subsequently, he sold it to the Beach Cattle Company.

Sada purchased the parcel two years later. When you think of pioneer women, Sada embodies that persona. She knew the value of the land and loved her ranch. For many years she raised Hereford cattle as well as other farm animals. She was also an accomplished poet and author. In 1953, she donated the Pine Ridge Ranch property to the county of Santa Clara in memory of her father, Henry Willard Coe. In 1958, a gift deed of 12,230 acres was given to the State of California for $10.00. This parcel became what is now Henry Coe State Park (east of Morgan Hill).

One of Sada's two daughters, Nancy remained in the family home after completely restoring it. She lived in The Villages for a short time before returning to the ranch. The ranch was renamed Rancho San Felipe and later became the Coe Ranch.

Rancho Yerba Buena

Taking a drive out Yerba Buena Road, beyond Evergreen College one finds a working cattle ranch. The sign reads Rancho Yerba Buena which is a remaining piece of the original Rancho that was granted to Antonio Chaboya. The Thompson family currently owns this ranch.

In 2010, I had the opportunity to visit Peggy Kuhn Thompson at The Ranch. She took me on an incredible ride in her *gator* up the wildflower laden hills that border on The Villages. When she turned off the engine, I had 360 degree views of beautiful rolling hills dotted with oak trees. As I looked down toward the valley, I saw The Villages spread out in front of me. From that vantage point I had this wonderful view of our community.

The following is a brief history written by Peggy Kuhn Thompson as they prepared to celebrate the 100th anniversary of the ranch.

"In 1833 Rancho Yerba Buena, one of the original California Spanish land grants was deeded to Don Antonio Chaboya. At that time, the Rancho covered 24,343 acres of the east Santa Clara County foothills. The house was built in 1865 on mud sills using timbers brought around the horn on a sailing ship. In 1875 Henry Pierce acquired 2.400 acres of the land, including the Grant's headquarters which kept the original title, Yerba Buena, meaning 'good grass'. In those days, tenant farmers grew peas, corn and dry beans on the hillsides, and Mr. Pierce raised dairy cows.

In 1910, bachelor Albert Charles Kuhn purchased the Ranch from the Pierce family. He remodeled the house, landscaped the grounds and ran beef cattle on the verdant hills. Upon his death, he willed the Ranch to his younger brother, Charles John Kuhn. The younger Kuhn married Edna Alwilda Bowman, daughter of a prominent San Jose businessman. They had two sons. In 1933, their elder son, Charles Bowman Kuhn (1910-1985) had just started his second year at Harvard Business School when his father died, prompting him to return home to run the Ranch. In addition to Hereford cattle, vineyards and fruit and nut orchards flourished on the "YB".

In 1950 C.B.K. married Edith Lyman of Westwood, MA; they had two daughters. Peggy Kuhn Thompson began running the Ranch when her father died in 1985. She has three children: Charles Kuhn Thompson, Blair Bowman Thompson and Frances Forbes Thompson. The rest of the story is still being written."

Another remnant of ranching, The Richmond Ranch, lies south, just beyond the last housing developments on San Felipe Road.

John Joseph Montgomery

A village, five streets, an elementary school and a hill are all named after this pioneer airman of Santa Clara County. Though he was not a landowner, John Montgomery had a major impact on this area of San José.

In 1883, at the age of 25, he became the first person in America to be supported freely in the air by a glider. At this time, he made and tested his first full scale glider by manning it and running it down long slopes in Otay, California which is in San Diego County.

John Montgomery was born in Yuba City, California. He received his degree from San Ignatius College in San Francisco in 1879, at which time he returned to his father's ranch in Otay, California. There was a delay in his aeronautical progress for a time while he managed his father's ranch. Those around him knew well of his interest in flight and electricity.

Montgomery's interest in flying never wavered. Though often taunted by friends, on August 28, 1883, with the help of his brother, James, he loaded his flying contraption into the farm wagon and covered it with hay to hide it from prying eyes. This enabled him to proceed, inconspicuously to his flying site for his experiments.

His original research was based on a study of birds and tests of models. Montgomery continued with studies on air flow over curved and cambered wings. He even presented a paper to a scientific group in Chicago on this subject.

In 1896, Montgomery returned to the Bay area where he taught Physics while pursuing his education at Santa Clara College (now known as Santa Clara University). He continued his experiments on model gliders which he flew off a railroad trestle in Santa Cruz.

In 1888 he made one of aviation's most important discoveries; the parabolic curved wing, that uses air flowing over the curve to create lift. This principle is still being used by all aeronautical engineers.

It was December 19, 1903 when Orville and Wilbur Wright flew their first powered airplane the Kitty Hawk, which was airborne for 12 seconds and traveled 120 feet.

Two years later, in 1905 Montgomery constructed a man-carrying tandem wing glider, named the Santa Clara which was lifted aloft by a hot air balloon. This glider lifted 4,000 feet off the ground, was released and came gliding down. It took eight minutes of skillful maneuvering before it landed on the ground about three quarters of a mile from the launching spot. He was accompanied on these tests by a man named Daniel Maloney. Maloney, a parachutist, was quite an attraction in the Bay area for his parachuting skills. After making several successful flights for Montgomery, in July of 1905, a release rope bent a strut of the glider and it crashed, killing Maloney. Montgomery temporarily put his experiments on hold after this tragedy.

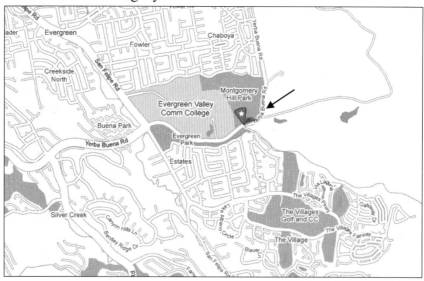

Then in 1906, just when he had another glider ready for testing, the large San Francisco earthquake destroyed his shop and gliders. Discouraged, he returned to teaching and creating other inventions.

The Evergreen courtesy San José History Museum

Six years later, again back to his flight experiments, he created a glider with wheels and control surfaces. He named this glider The Evergreen. He began flights in Evergreen Valley from the crest of a hill behind the current location of Evergreen College north of The Villages. This area is now known as Montgomery Hill Park which was donated to the city of San José by Charles Kuhn.

In the early 1960's, Richard Neiman, who lived on San Felipe Road visited Charles Kuhn with a photograph in his hand. The photograph was of one of the flights of Montgomery. He said, "Charles, look at this picture of John Montgomery flying. Based on the shape of the hill and the location of the trees, I think he flew on your hill." It was as a result of this discovery that Charles Kuhn gave a section of his ranch where the hill was situated, for the above mentioned park.

Montgomery made about fifty flights at this location, until October 31, 1911 when experiencing some dizziness, he made a rough landing. So rough that the glider flipped over and Montgomery's head struck a protruding bolt which penetrated his brain, resulting in his death.

His success was celebrated with a John J. Montgomery Day which included a small parade. In 1967, the State Department of Parks and Recreation of Santa Clara County erected a marker with a plaque in John Montgomery's honor. The plaque which was on the Evergreen College site, states: "Three quarters of a mile northeast is Montgomery Hill, site of fifty-five successful flights of the aeroplane of John Joseph Montgomery which demonstrated aerodynamic developments indispensible to modern aircraft. Here the basic principles of aerodynamics discovered by Montgomery were combined by his engineering skill and technology to produce a heavier than air flying machine which had complete control: the cambered wing, rear stabilizer, flexible wing tips and the wing-warping aileron."

Nationally, honors were bestowed on Montgomery. In 1964, he was inducted into the National Aviation Hall of Fame followed in 2002 with induction into the U.S. Soaring Hall of Fame. In 1996 the American Society of Mechanical Engineers recognized Montgomery's 1883 glider as an International Historical Engineering Landmark.

The construction of a small park in 2008, on the corner of San Felipe Road and Yerba Buena Road is a testimony to the success of John Joseph Montgomery. There is a metal wing structure in the park commemorating his work with the airflow over curved wings. The aforementioned plaque was moved to the new location.

In 1971, a village was named for him at The Villages in San José, CA. Within that village are five streets; Montgomery Lane, Montgomery Bend, Montgomery Corner, Montgomery Court, and Montgomery Place. There is also a street by Reed-Hillview airport, also in San José, appropriately named Montgomery.

The W.R.C. Home of Evergreen

The National Women's Relief Corps (W.R.C.) was founded in Denver, Colorado in 1883; an auxiliary to the Grand Army of the Republic (GAR). The GAR was a fraternal organization of the Union Army that fought in the Civil War.

The W.R.C. had a three-fold mission statement; "to assist in preserving and making available for research, documents and records pertaining to the Grand Army of the Republic and its members; to assist Veterans of all wars of the United States and to extend needful aid to their widows and orphans; and to maintain allegiance to the United States of America by inoculating lessons of patriotism and love of country among the children and communities in which they live and encourage the spread of universal liberty and equal rights of all".

Six years later, in 1889, the first W.R.C. Home in the nation was built in Evergreen. The establishment of this home was to provide shelter for the widows and orphans of the Civil War Union veterans. Mr. Nirum Cadwallader donated five acres of land for the home. Miss Mineola Wheeler was matron of the home from 1899 until 1902 when she married John Hassler.

While serving as matron, there were some concerns that Miss Wheeler, due to her young age, would not be able to make the hired help obey instructions. That was apparently not a problem, as she handled the position very well. There were many social functions at the *Home* such as luncheons, a *sing* and frequent visitors.

The home was destroyed by fire in 1920. In 1956, the Grand Army of the Republic was dissolved. Its records went to the Library of Congress in Washington, D.C.

The W.R.C. is the oldest women's patriotic organization in the United States and still exists today.

Even after the construction of The Villages had begun; this old farmhouse was a landmark as one entered Villages Parkway. Owned by Mr. and Mrs. Enos, this remnant of the early settlers was part of the vivid memories of children who had been raised in the area. It was under consideration as an historical landmark, but the house was demolished in 1987.

Many of these former accounts are remnants of days gone by and some are still there for us to enjoy. Time does move on, but a blending of the old and the new always makes a more complete picture of an area and in this case the section of San José known as Evergreen.

William Gottlieb Wehner

As we turn the clock back to the end of the nineteenth century, the parcel of land that we know as The Villages has again changed ownership as well as acreage. In 1887, a portion of the Rancho Yerba Buena was purchased by William Gottlieb Wehner, an immigrant from Hanover, Germany. His piece of property was located on the western slope of the hills and he considered it good farmland due to many living springs that supplied an excellent source of water. Two that were tapped, yielded 8,000 to 20,000 gallons of water per day.

Wehner soon began developing his newly acquired land. At this time, James Lick, Leland Stanford and James Phelen were prominent leaders in the Santa Clara Valley and Grover Cleveland was president of the United States.

Wehner arrived in the United States in 1865 at the age of 18 and settled in Chicago, Illinois. He was naturalized in 1883 stating at that time that he had been a farmer in Germany. It would be 30 years later that he returned to farming. When first arriving in the United States, he operated a crockery store. He was also an accomplished artist who became well known for his large painted panoramas that are hanging in major cities across the country. (Indianapolis, Detroit, Chicago, and Buffalo) The most celebrated are The Crucifixion of Christ, The Battle of Gettysburg and Missionary Ridge.

William married Elizabeth Marie Stutza while living in Chicago. They had one daughter, Ida.

One of his eleven siblings, a brother Ernest also emigrated from Germany and settled in San José, working as a tinsmith. After Wehner purchased the Evergreen property, he convinced his brother to join him planting grapes and fruit

29

trees. Ernest planted over 300 acres with 175 imported grape varieties. Prior to the grapes, they planted an extensive orchard of choice fruit trees on 50 acres, which included apricots, 500 nectarines, 200 peaches, 500 French prunes, 500 Bartlett pears, almonds and some oranges.

While William Wehner was planting grape vines in preparation for the production of wine, Carrie Nation was working feverishly in Kansas to abolish the consumption of alcohol and forming The Women's Christian Temperance Union.

Wehner hired the prestigious firm of Burnham and Root from Chicago to design his Evergreen home in 1888. This firm also designed the Flatiron building in New York City, the Monadnock and Rookery buildings in Chicago, the old Chronicle building and the Mills buildings in San Francisco and the Union Station in Washington, D.C.

The home was completed in 1891 at a cost of $20,000. Wehner named his home Lomas Azules (Blue Hills) His home, referred to as The Mansion today, is a Queen Anne style with three stories. The construction was of wood and stone, the latter coming from a quarry in nearby hills. Central heating did not exist when the home was built; therefore the house has eight fireplaces. Mrs. Wehner brought her own plumber from Chicago to install a bathroom. Indoor plumbing did not become available, generally until after 1900. There is an enclosed sun porch with a balcony above, which is accessed from the master bedroom. The house has a full basement with a wine cellar.

An article in the San José Daily Mercury in 1901 said, "The ranch is one of the many beautiful country homes in the valley...it is the finest and most beautiful vineyard in California."

On October 17, 1989, the Wehner Mansion was designated an Historic Landmark Building by the City of San José. It has been nominated for the National Registry, but not formally listed.

On the estate were some outbuildings; a summer kitchen and a cottage. Many magnificent trees lined the drive leading to the house that included palms, magnolias, firs and a giant monkey puzzle tree.

Driving up the Olive tree bordered main road, you passed through a massive stone gate that was the entrance to the mansion. The gate still stands in its original location, which today is on the golf course by the ninth tee.

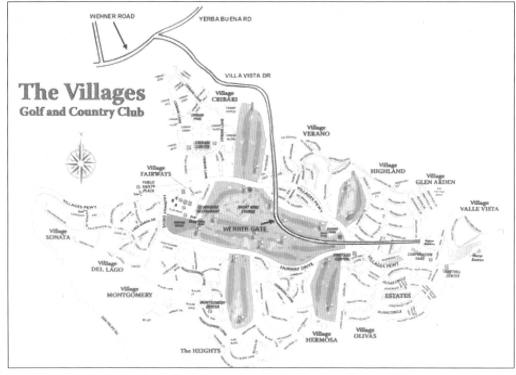

Overlay of Wehner Road and Villa Vista Road circa 1910
Map courtesy of The Villages Golf and Country Club 2010

For a short time, around 1910, the portion of the road from San Felipe Road to Villa Vista Road was named Wehner Road. (see map above) It is currently named Yerba Buena Road.

Garden party at the Wehner home c.1900

Using the name of Highland Vineyards, Wehner produced premium wines under his own label. He perfected the process of cool fermentation of white wine and as a result his sauternes were rated the finest in California. They continued to receive the highest evaluations for 25 years. Charles Sullivan, in his book "Like Modern Edens", described Wehner as the "most important individual in regional winegrowing 1905 - 1915". The red grape varieties that were grown were: Cabernet Sauvignon, Cabernet France, Saint Macaire, Petite Pinot, Zinfandel of Austria, Carignan of France, and Mataro of Spain. The white varieties were; Sauvignon Blanc, Sauvignon Vert, Folle Blanc, Semillone, German Riesling, Burger and Gutedel.

In 1901 when most of the smaller wineries were on the verge of bankruptcy, William Wehner produced 200,000 gallons of wine. Wehner had good business sense. That and scientific management helped him survive the economic crisis of the late 1800's and the grapevine blight, Phylloxera (a small sap-sucking insect that is a pest of grapevines worldwide) that followed the financial crisis. When Mr. Wehner was complimented on the abundance and luxury of his grapes and wines, he said, "We don't take things by chance here. Our motto is that a thing worth doing is worth doing right and at the right time".

Wehner Ranch

1 Main Residence
2 Summer Kitchen
3 Garden House
4 Rock Wall
5 Brick Path
6 1908 Winery
7 Boiler House
8 Winery Office
9 Garage
10 1890 Winery
11 Bunkhouse
12 High Barn
13 Low Fruit Barn
14 Residential Buildings/Office
15 Residential Building

Map courtesy of Ruth & Going, Inc. 1986

Visitors to the
Wehner Ranch

There were several additional outbuildings associated with the old winery. One of these was an 1890 winery building. It used the force of gravity to move the crushed grapes to the fermenting tanks. There were also a few barns. A larger winery building made of stone and redwood was built in 1908. It had a storage capacity of 500,000 gallons of cooperage. The winery serviced 475 acres of grapes. The building was later used by Cribari, Mirassou and Paul Masson wineries to cellar their wines.

Winery circa 1890 Courtesy of The Villages Golf and Country Club

Bunkhouses for the vineyard workers were scattered along the hillside.

Photo courtesy of Betty Stednitz

A road by the mansion went over a deep ravine (current location is near Foothill Center) and a wooden bridge was suspended over the ravine.

William Wehner sold the property, including an additional 80 acres north of the original 718 acres to Albert Haentze in 1915. At that time, Wehner moved to a home on E. Santa Clara Street in San José. After selling the remainder of the property; the winery and ranch in 1925, he and his family moved to Palo Alto with the intent of pursuing his interest in art and culture. He died there in February 1928 at the age of 80. His wife, Elizabeth died in 1933 at the age of 82. Their one daughter, Ida worked as a secretary for Jane Lathrup Stanford who was co-founder of Stanford University in Palo Alto.

William Wehner with his two dogs in a late 1903 Autocar.

Photos courtesy of The Villages Golf and Country Club

Albert Haentze

Villa Vista Vineyard c.1915   courtesy of Jerry Smith

Albert Haentze was born in Wisconsin and was heavily involved in real estate in Chicago, Illinois before moving to California. He married Lillie Richardson and they had a daughter, Irene.

Albert E. Haentze, who presided at the Santa Clara County meetings.

Courtesy of Wines and Vines Magazine

In 1915, Albert Haentze purchased the Lomas Azules Mansion and 651 acres of land north of the creek from William Wehner. Wehner retained the winery and the property south of the creek.

By this time, Irene was married to Walter Pierce and they had one son, Albert Jerome. The marriage ended and Irene moved with her young son onto her parents' estate and lived in the cottage.

Albert Jerome Haentze III   (on the right)

After the early death of Irene, Albert Sr. adopted Albert Jerome and gave him the surname of Haentze. Albert Jerome Haentze, Jr. married Anne Marie Hannon and they had one son, Albert Jerome Haentze, III.

In order to create his own stamp on the mansion, Haentze renamed it Rancho Villa Vista. The winery remained Villa Vista Vineyard as named by Wehner.

Haentze was an executive of many years experience in large business and finance. After doing extensive re-search and study he made the decision to carry on the same general plan and principles as Mr. Wehner. Haentze made some further purchases of adjoining properties and did additional planting on the land. He also made many improvements to the buildings and the ranch. As a result, he was credited at the time as having one of the best-equipped and maintained di-

Albert Haentze

versified ranches in the state of California.

Mr. Haentze succeeded as a leader of the Santa Clara Valley grape growers. He was chairman of the Deciduous Association, as well as being actively involved with the Vineyardists' Association, the Wine Institute and the California Grape Growers Exchange of which he became their first president. He was also the first president of the California Wine Advisory Board.

A quote from *Wine and Vines Magazine*, "Like Mr. Wehner, he (Haentze), too, is imbued and inoculated with the spirit and romance of fine wine production. Thus there is every assurance that the fame and name and quality of Villa Vista Vineyard vines will be maintained for the enjoyment of those who partake." The wines Haentze produced were; California Burgundy, California Sauterne, California Sweet Sauterne, California Riesling and California Cabernet.

Unfortunately, Haentze fought a losing battle with the forces of prohibition in 1920 and along with most of the wineries in the area, the winery was closed. Prohibition was a result of the Women's Christian Temperance movement led by Frances Willard and supported by Wayne Wheeler, putting pressure on the United States Senate until the 18th amendment was ratified in 1919. There was of course opposition to the act by wine producers and ads began appearing in magazines and newspapers. The prohibition law went into effect in January 1920. The Volstead Act, (the popular name for the Na-

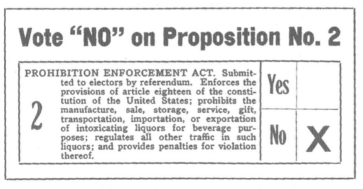

Vote "NO" on Proposition No. 2

| 2 | PROHIBITION ENFORCEMENT ACT. Submitted to electors by referendum. Enforces the provisions of article eighteen of the constitution of the United States; prohibits the manufacture, sale, storage, service, gift, transportation, importation, or exportation of intoxicating liquors for beverage purposes; regulates all other traffic in such liquors; and provides penalties for violation thereof. | Yes | |
| | | No | X |

tional Prohibition Act) was passed by Congress over President Woodrow Wilson's veto. Andrew Volstead was Chairman of the House Judiciary Committee, which oversaw its passage. 10,000 gallons of wine were dumped into New York Harbor in 1923. The Volstead Act prohibited the sale of alcohol, but little was done to enforce the law. In New York City alone, there were more than 30,000 speakeasy clubs. During the Great Depression, prohibition became increasingly unpopular. President Franklin Roosevelt signed an amendment to the Volstead Act allowing the manufacture and sale of some kinds of alcoholic beverages. On December 5, 1933, the ratification of the 21st Amendment repealed the 18th Amendment.

That same year, the University of California purchased the Haentze vineyard and used it for viniculture. After considering the site for another campus for the university, they chose a Santa Cruz location.

Courtesy of Jerry Smith

After the sale, Haentze's son, Albert Haentze, Jr. stayed at the property as the manager of the Villa Vista Vineyards. In March of 1940, according to the *San José News*, he was driving a car with Joe Coehlo, an employee of the winery. Haentze crashed into the stone gate on the property and was crushed. Coehlo survived the crash. Haentze was survived by his wife, Anne, son, Albert and his grandparents Mr. and Mrs. Albert Haentze.

Sorting and cutting cots

A large part of the estate was devoted to an apricot orchard. Financially, at the time, the apricots were more successful than the wine produced at Villa Vista.

The location of Villa Vista Road today would run right through the golf course, adjacent to the second green and along the first part of the third hole. (Map in the Wehner chapter) Originally, this was the main road from Yerba Buena Road to the mansion and the entrance to the property until Villages Parkway was constructed in 1967.

The Mirassou Family

The Mirassou family began growing grapes and producing highly rated wines in the eastern foothills of San José in 1854. They are known to be America's oldest winemaking family.

The history of the Mirassou Winery begins with Louis Pellier who came to California in 1849. He established a nursery in San José. His brother, Pierre Pellier sailed from France with his bride, Henrietta, arriving here in 1851. He brought with him some cuttings of his prized grape vines. These were the first Pinot Noir grapes in California. During this sailing, water became scarce on the ship, so being very inventive, Pierre purchased potatoes; inserted his cuttings, thereby keeping his vines alive.

Pierre and Henrietta Pellier

Courtesy of Wines and Vines Magazine

Pierre purchased and operated over 300 acres in the eastern foothills of San José, known as the Evergreen Valley and developed his winery in 1854. Louis Pellier joined him and managed the winery until his brother's death in 1872.

Pierre's daughter, also named Henrietta married a neighboring vineyardist, Pierre Mirassou. Mirassou and Pellier became partners in what was going to prove to be an extremely successful winegrowing operation. Pierre and Henrietta Mirassou had three sons before Pierre died in 1889. Their sons, Peter, John and Herman were teenagers when they inherited the winery. A neighbor, Thomas Casalegno was a successful rancher and business man who helped them with the winery until the Mirassou boys were knowledgeable themselves.

Casalegno was instrumental in developing a grafting process for grape vines to combat the devastating small insect, Phylloxera, which was destroying the vineyards in Europe. The American grape stocks were resistant to this bug, but the quality of the wine was poor. Casalegno traded American root stock for cuttings of the European grape vines. He then grafted the cuttings to the American root stock, thereby producing some very fine grapes. This was also a successful solution for the European Vineyardists, as they took the American root stock and also did grafting. Henrietta married one of the Casalegno sons, Thomas.

The original Mirassou Winery was on Chaboya Road near Quimby Road in Evergreen. Their second winery was located on the corner of White Road and Quimby Road where a shopping center is now situated. Another winery was north of the present location of Evergreen College on Yerba Buena Road.

As with all the wineries in the area, the prohibition years took their toll. The Mirassou Vineyard survived through these years under the supervision of Peter Mirassou and his wife Justine. Peter's two brothers sold out their portion of the vineyard to Peter, feeling that it was hopeless to continue under the restrictive conditions of prohibition. Peter was able to keep the business solid by selling grapes at markets from Chicago to New York. Many families in the east were making their 200 gallons per year of wine, allowed under the prohibition law, and needed the grapes. Since a large number of vineyardists were tearing out their grapevines, Mirassou had an increasingly large market. They also sold their wine for sacramental and medicinal uses until prohibition ended in 1933.

Mirassou having the largest crop of grapes in the area also sold them to the Cribari Winery. Of all the growers that Cribari bought from, Mirassou was the largest. Mirassou was selling about four loads a day, each one weighing about 10 tons. After quite a few years, the Bisceglias, a large wine producing family, opened a winery in San José and there was concern that they would run everybody else out of business. Fortunately there was enough business for everyone.

In 1937, Mirassou traded some property in the Evergreen area for the property on Aborn Road. Two years later they built the first stage of their winery. In 1938, they sold the vintage 1937 to Cribari at 10 cents a gallon. The University of California (U.C.) owned the property south of the Mirassou Winery and they approached Mirassou about running their ranch for them. Mirassou agreed.

Norbert and Edmond

From about 1940 - 1945 Norbert Mirassou operated the old winery north of the Wehner Mansion as well as the entire ranch of apricots, prunes and walnuts. Norbert, his wife and daughter lived in the mansion for those four years.

About this time, the Cribari family also purchased land from U.C. About two years later, U.C. again approached Mirassou about purchasing more property that they were now interested in selling. The Cribari family had already offered to purchase it, but U.C. thought Mirassou should have the first option as they had been working the land already. Mirassou declined the U.C. offer.

The number of orchards and vineyards was increasing and, as a result, water had become scarce in the Evergreen area. The Mirassous dug many wells which they used for irrigation. In the late 1950's the Santa Clara Valley Conservation District brought a canal from Anderson Reservoir to the Evergreen area which significantly increased the water supply. This was a cooperative pipeline that the Mirassous shared with their neighbors. As homes began to replace the many orchards, water usage decreased.

In 1961, Edmond Mirassou (the great-grandson of Pierre Pellier and owner of Mirassou vineyards) moved south and chose Monterey County as an ideal climate for further grape culture. He pioneered grape growing along the Central Coast of California. Edmond received the Merit Award, the highest honor given by the American Society for Enology and Viticulture in 1979. This presentation was awarded for his many good works in the wine industry. He also served as chairman of the Wine Advisory Board.

The Mirassou Vineyards matured, the crop harvests increased and there was a need for more storage space for the wine. The fifth generation of the Mirassou family, Daniel, Peter and Jim were now running the whole operation. In an agreement with The

44

Villages Golf and Country Club in 1974, Mirassou Winery leased the property (formerly the Cribari Winery) which was two miles away from their Aborn Road operation. They used the property for storage and ageing of their wines. They purchased all the equipment and casks that had been used by the former Cribari Winery.

There were enough redwood and oak casks to hold more than 500,000 gallons of wine for aging. Mirassou used the facility for storage until 1994.

In 2002, E. & J. Gallo purchased the Mirassou name and continued the wine production under the same labels. The property remained in the family trust. Daniel, Peter and Jim Mirassou produced a new brand called *La Rochelle*. In 2003, La Rochelle wines were sold to the Steven Kent (Mirassou) Winery in Livermore.

This fifth generation of Mirassou; Daniel, Jim and Peter continued the family tradition until 2005. The sixty-eight year old estate owned by the Mirassou family once spread over 350 acres, but most of the land has since been developed for residential use and only 15 acres of winery buildings and vineyards remain.

Courtesy Wines and Vines Magazine

After 150 years, on September 1, 2005, La Rochelle's (formerly Mirassou) tasting room on Aborn Road closed.

Beniamino Cribari, Fondatore
Cribari Winery

The Cribari Family

Benjamino (Benjamin) Cribari, the founder of Cribari Wines, was a native of the village of Aprigliano in Calabria province, Italy, where he learned the trade of viticulture from his relatives.

He was married to Josephine Abruzzini. His four sons; Fiore, Angelo, Stanislaus and Anthony were born in Italy, and his three daughters; Irma, Mary and Helen were born in the United States after he moved to San José. As with many Italians around 1900, he immigrated to Canada. Italy was getting very crowded and Garibaldi, a major military and political leader in Italy at that time, was conscripting the young men. As a result, many Italians came, to North America in order to escape the draft. After his arrival, Benjamin worked on the Canadian Pacific Railroad.

Fiore Cribari

World communication was poor or non-existent at that time. A strike occurred with the railroad in 1896. Benjamin seized the opportunity to make a visit to Italy because of concerns about his family's welfare. When he returned to Canada, he brought his eldest son, Fiore with him. Fiore worked as a water boy on the railroad, during the summer. During the school year, he went to school in Spokane, Washington. After a second strike, Benjamin and Fiore moved to Trinidad, Colorado to work in the coalmines. He then sent for his wife and the three younger sons.

Benjamin knew the coalmines were not a good choice of a place to raise his sons. Having some relatives in San José, California, and hearing of work opportunities, Benjamin relocated in 1902. Benjamin began his new career as a farmer by pruning trees and vines in the orchards for $1.50 a day. All his sons worked with him picking fruit. Upon receiving the money from the sale of his house in Italy, he went to Paradise Valley (southwest of Morgan Hill) and bought forty acres of hillside land to plant his first grape orchard. He bought a horse and a two-wheeled cart and with his sons, cleared the land and built a wine cellar and a house. His entrepreneurial nature led him to sell tree trunks and oak roots for firewood, as well as making charcoal.

When the land was ready for planting, he took the entire family to the hillside, knelt and blessed himself, dug a hole and planted the first grape vine which he had obtained from his neighbors. He said, "Now, boys, this is the first planting but with God's help we will plant and have many more". Benjamin's prayers were answered. By the time he died in 1942, he had developed more than one thousand acres of Cribari vineyards and four wineries.

His sons remembered his father buying them new boots, cutting a barrel in half, putting in some freshly picked grapes and saying, "Jump in and dance on the grapes."

Courtesy of wines and Vines Magazine

The Cribari family expanded their business with a winery in New York as well as those in California. At their New York location in the Bronx, Benjamin hosted many groups for dinner and wine-tasting in the wine cellar, called The Cellar in the Sky. The owner of the Hofbrau Restaurant on Broadway suggested to Benjamin that it would be an ideal location to host dinners for restaurateurs and introduce them to Cribari wines. Amongst the large oak barrels, long tables were set up. The guests and the host all donned monk's attire and enjoyed a fine meal accompanied by Cribari wine.

Courtesy of Claire Tearse

Angelo G. Cribari

Two of Benjamin's sons, Angelo and Anthony went to work at the Bisceglia Brothers Cannery on 1st Street in San José. As told to his family, Angelo remembered putting the lids on the cans with a spool of lead in one hand and a soldering iron in the other. This cannery was the largest in the United States and the canned goods were sold internationally. Both Angelo and Stanislaus served their new country during World War I, with Stanislaus losing his life. Fiore continued to work with his father. After marrying Marietta Bisceglia he bought his own small winery (Estrada Winery) in Madrone, south of San José.

The Bisceglia family's roots were in southern Italy in the same town as the Cribaris. Clementina Bisceglia married Thomas Cribari, Benjamin's brother. They also immigrated to Canada about 1900, where they worked on the Canadian Pacific Railroad laying tracks in Western Canada. The Bisceglias; Thomas, Clementina and their five children gradually moved south into California until they found a climate similar to that in Italy which was the Berryessa section of San José. They broke horses for work and received their payment is land located in Paradise Valley, near Uvas.

After settling in Paradise Valley, they planted alternating rows of grapes and tomatoes on the land. This activity expanded to planting acres of fruits and vegetables near Pacheco Pass. The enterprise became the Casa de Fruita that is still in operation today. Photo below is a Bisceglia Cannery peach label.

With the financial help of A.P. Giannini and the Bank of Italy, they opened a cannery in Gilroy. As the business grew; they built a larger one in Morgan Hill and eventually a cannery and winery in San José on 1st Street, which they operated for many years.

Bisceglia Cannery Gilroy 1909

Mention must be made here of A.P. Giannini who founded the Bank of Italy in San José, which became the Bank of America in 1928. He played a very important role in helping the Italian immigrants who arrived in San José. Giannini was born in San José and at a young age was delivering vegetables and fruit from San José to San Francisco for his step-father's business. Giannini eventually built his own very successful business and as a result was asked to serve on the board of directors of the Columbus Savings and Loan Society. With his experience as a board member, he went on to establish the Bank of Italy. His motivation came from seeing the poor treatment given to immigrants. As mentioned above, he helped the Bisceglias as well as other people starting in the wine industry. In 1923 he created a motion picture loan division and helped the movie industry including Walt Disney.

The Bisceglia family built a beautiful home on Monterey Road known as Casa Grande where everyone in the Bisceglia family lived at one time.

About 1925, the Bisceglias purchased a parcel of the land from Albert Haentze and nurtured the grapes that were growing there. This land was the eastern portion of the Haentze estate. They continued the grape growing on the Evergreen property and crushed, stored and bottled the wine at their winery on First Street until the late 1930's.

In our family, wine-making has been a tradition for three generations, started by my grandfather, Beniamino. When he arrived from the old country he brought with him the skills of the Italian winemakers, whose pride has always been Spumante, the sparkling wine we save for celebrations. I'm offering this commemorative Spumante as a special tribute to my grandfather and to the traditions he has shared with all of us. Saluto! — Albert B. Cribari

B. Cribari

Gradually, the Cribaris acquired more land along with their wineries in San Benito County, San Joaquin County and Santa Clara County, as well as one in New York State. They were shipping grapes across the country in railroad tank cars with the words, *The House of Cribari* on the side. B. Cribari and sons were producing about three million gallons of wine a year. They refrigerated the grapes for transport by using ice from Lake Tahoe, where most of the region's ice was produced at the time.

B. Cribari & Son, of San Jose, shipped nine cars of grapes—about 140 tons of Zinfandel, Alicante Bouschet and Muscats—on the steel motor-ship "Kennecott," which sailed from San Francisco on Sept. 22nd via the Canal and is due in New York on October 15th. The picture above shows the lidded lugs being loaded in a huge compartment in the center of the vessel. Later this was made air-tight and treated with carbon dioxide gas.

World War I had ended and it was followed by 13 years of prohibition which were devastating for the wineries. Many closed down. The Cribari Winery survived, by selling and shipping the grapes, grape juice and grape syrup to small wine producing families on the east coast who were making wine at home.

B. CRIBARI & SONS, Inc.

HOME OFFICE: SAN JOSE   BRANCHES: NEW YORK

Bottled Sunshine — Mellowed By Age

LAS PALMAS, SAN BENITO, ST. CLAIRE BRANDS

Customers would purchase what were called blocks or bricks of wine. On the outside of the packaging, the label would read i.e., "Block of Port Wine. After dissolving brick in a gallon of water, do not place the jug away in the cupboard for twenty days, because it will turn into wine." They received permission from the Prohibition Bureau to add excess salt to sherry and sell it in gallon jugs as cooking wine. Port wine was sweetened with excess sugar and sold to bakers and restaurants. They also sold their wine to churches and synagogues for sacramental use. When prohibition was repealed in 1933, the Cribaris had a quarter million gallons of aged wine in their wineries in California and New York.

They had several different brands; Sonny Boy named for Angelo's son, Las Palmas named after the Cribari winery in Fresno and Saint Claire named after Angelo's daughter, Claire.

SONNIE BOY BRAND

B. CRIBARI & SONS
1066 BIRD AVE., SAN JOSE, CAL.
Phone: San Jose 3937

SHIPPERS OF BEST CALIFORNIA GRAPES
REG. U.S. PAT. OFF.

Courtesy of Wines and Vines Magazine

Following prohibition, the individual states had the choice of whether or not to liberalize their laws. Many states chose not to do that, but fortunately for the Cribari family both New York and California did liberalize their laws which encouraged the resurgence of the wine industry. This period was followed by the Great Depression, but the California wineries survived probably due to the change in the law.

Always looking for business opportunities, Cribari sold wine to a cigar making company, strange as that may sound. The owner of the cigar company would come and taste the wine and determine when the taste was perfect according to his liking. He used the wine to coat the tobacco leaves before rolling them into a cigar.

By 1937, Cribari wines had achieved some notoriety. *Wines and Vines Magazine* stated, "The Waldorf Astoria in New York City, which has been a hard nut to crack, due to their importing of foreign wines, has at last given up and is now listing the San Benito wines on their wine list". The Society of Restaurateurs who has a reputation of a fine high-class trade business also endorsed their wines.

In 1941, the country was again engaged in a World War with the bombing of Pearl Harbor. Many young men went off to fight in the war which put a strain on the work force at home.

Benjamin, Angelo and Fiore's wife, Marietta died in 1942. That same year, B. Cribari and Sons purchased the eastern portion of the former Haentze estate and winery from the Bank of America, who had acquired the property from The University of California. In 1945, they purchased the western half which included the mansion. Fiore married Violet Couts and they moved into the mansion and renamed it The Ranch or Villa Vista. They named the mile long drive from the gate to the mansion Olive Lane because of the olives trees that lined it on both sides. The mansion had been empty for most of the 10 years during the time that the university owned it and the Cribaris needed to do a great deal of restoration. They also did some remodeling which included the addition of three more bathrooms. World War II had just ended and new furniture was difficult to find, so Violet Cribari and her sister-in-law, Zoe went to auction halls to find suitable furniture for this huge home.

Cribari replaced the grape vines at the Evergreen site with Pinot Blanc, Chenin Blanc, Grigliano, Petite Syrah, Carignan and Green Hungarian. There were extensive storage capabilities in the huge oak barrels in the barn. The bottling was done at the Madrone location for the west coast and New York for the east coast. The hillside land was leased to the McConnell family for cattle grazing.

Besides Mirassou; Paul Masson, Sebastiani, Guild and Gallo wineries did not have the quantity of grapes for the wine production that they needed, and also purchased grapes from the Cribari family.

The Mansion was the site of many parties while the Cribaris were in residence. Some of these parties included well-known movie personalities. After a Circle Theater Youth benefit, guests and performers came to Villa Vista for cocktails and supper. Included at the event were; Frank Sinatra, Rory Calhoun, Rhonda Fleming, Dennis Morgan, Jack Carson, Buddy Baer.

In 1955 the Cribaris merged the San Joaquin operation with the Alta Vineyard in Fresno. Cribari sold off 1,000 acres which included the original Evergreen property to Alexander C. Ganiats and Earl R. Mason in 1959. The latter defaulted on the purchase and it went to the Bank of America until Guy Atkinson Company purchased the property in 1966. Shortly after, Cribari leased the property back, including the ranch, winery and all the vineyards.

In the meantime, construction of The Villages began by Atkinson-Mackay. Anthony (Tony) Cribari managed the now shrinking vineyard in Evergreen until Atkinson needed the remainder of the property for construction. Tony and his wife, Zoe moved into Cribari Village and enjoyed many happy years in the community.

Anthony Cribari

After about 90 years of grape cultivation and wine making, the use of Rancho Yerba Buena changed dramatically. Technology was moving very quickly and the urban sprawl in this part of California was significant. Gradually, the rolling hills were filled with the increasing multitude of homes. A need for homes for retired people became evident. The dream of building a community like The Villages which blended in with the environment, as well as preserving a natural setting gradually became reality.

Tony Cribari
is waiting for The Villages

Mr. Cribari has a number of reasons to wait for this new adult community. He is well aware of the vintage climate of Evergreen Valley after growing grapes for many years on the site that will be The Villages. It has been and will once again be "home" for this well known vintner. Mr. Cribari had this to say about the location, and The Villages: "On business trips I've visited every state and every key city at different times of the year, and none can compare with the beauty, climate and convenience of the Evergreen Valley. It's minutes from downtown San Jose, yet secluded from the hustle and bustle of the city. My wife and I decided on The Villages not just for sentimental reasons, but because it offered us a spacious and attractive condominium Villa, complete recreational, cultural, social and medical facilities and all the advantages of year-round, no maintenance living. With more free time, we're looking forward to a number of pleasure trips that have been planned." 鬼 A scale model of the first Village, Village Cribari, is on display in the temporary information center at the site. This center is open daily from 10 a.m. to 6 p.m. See this new concept in adult living by taking Highway 101 to the Capitol Expressway east turnoff, right on Aborn Road and follow the signs.

THE VILLAGES

THE VILLAGES
P.O. Box 6101
San Jose, California 95150

Please send me more information on The Villages

Name:_____

Address:_____

City:_____ Zip:_____

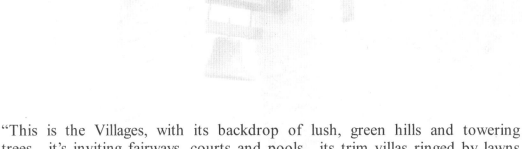

"This is the Villages, with its backdrop of lush, green hills and towering trees…it's inviting fairways, courts and pools…its trim villas ringed by lawns and lakes…its virgin uplands welcoming hiking and contemplation.

This is The Villages, with clubhouses for arts and crafts, for study and recreation, for gracious dining. But aside from the amenities, The Villages is much, much more. From far and wide the Villagers have come, bringing with them a diversity of mores. Here they have blended into a unique community of friendship and goodwill, evidenced in the greetings among the stroller, waves from cars and carts, the camaraderie at the business offices, the Villager sanctum, Post Office, Pro-Shop…in the dedication of directors and managers to the general welfare, in security, speeding to aid the stricken, in volunteers ministering to the ill and bereaved. This is indeed a blessed spot, a haven of nurturing for the body as well as repose for the spirit.
Truly a place apart…This is The Villages.

Jessie Levine

The Villages Golf and Country Club

Aerial view of The Villages c.1970

"Throughout the 1960's, 1970's and 1980's, the landscape of the Santa Clara Valley experienced a dramatic transformation. Orchards were steadily replaced by business and research parks and housing developments. The agriculture industry gave way to high technology enterprises that earned Silicon Valley its name. During this time, the valley lost over 500,000 acres of fruit and nut trees to the Central Valley and other regions of California."

Into this changing picture emerged a senior retirement community called The Villages. Nestled at the base of the eastern foothills, on a section of the former Rancho Yerba Buena, the vision of a few men came to fruition. The sloping hills were covered with grape vines, oak trees and olive trees. This was country living, a short distance from the developing commercialism of the city of San José.

In 1966, the Guy F. Atkinson Company joined with Mackay Homes and purchased the parcel of land now known as The Villages. The newly formed Atkinson-Mackay Corporation was re-named the Villages Management Corporation (VMC). Robert A. Nelson was appointed General Manager of The Villages on

September 1, 1966. At that time there were only some conceptual plans on paper. This was Atkinson's first venture into home building. Atkinson Construction was a major force in the construction industry worldwide. Locally, to name a few, they were involved in the San Francisco Airport, Junipero Serra Freeway, Lexington and Anderson Dams, the Oakland Coliseum and the Stanford Linear Accelerator Center.

The first major community building was Cribari Center which was built in 1967. On August 21, 1967, VMC moved into its new offices located in Cribari Center. The location of their office was in the room where the library is housed today (2010). They worked without electricity until September 12 and their telephone service until September 16, 1967.

John Mackay, San José Mayor Ron James, California Lt. Governor Robert Finch, Thomas Henderson (Atkinson-Mackay)

Lieutenant Governor Robert H. Finch formally dedicated Cribari Center on May 4, 1968. He was assisted by San José Mayor, Ronald R. James. Lieutenant Governor Finch gave a short address saying, "Here in the historic Cribari Vineyards, Atkinson and Mackay have preserved the spaciousness and naturalness of the early California days with its Spanish flavor and have sought to provide a good living for Californians in a vibrant and balanced way."

Mr. and Mrs. Tony Cribari, for whose family the first of the villages had been named, were honored guests at the dedication.

The rest of the center opened shortly after the VMC moved in. It housed some amenities for the use of the future residents. One of these amenities was the library which opened in January 1968. At that time, the library was a branch of the San José City Library. It was located in the balcony overlooking Cribari auditorium.

The library operated on an honor system without any librarians to assist or check out books. As a gesture of good will, Western Federal Savings donated books to the library on a regular basis.

In 1989 the library relocated to its present location in Cribari Center facing the west parking lot. It currently houses approximately 1,600 hard bound fiction books and 800 non-fiction books. In addition there are about 3,000 paperback books. The extensive collection of videos numbers about 200 and audio CD's and tapes about 250. Within these library walls, besides the above, are newspaper and magazine subscriptions, encyclopedias and jigsaw puzzles. There is also a group of helpful librarians who keep the books organized and current. In 2010, a computer was added for the residents' use.

The preview opening of The Villages was held on September 23 and 24, 1967. There were 75 visitors on Saturday and 1,150 on Sunday. The first resident, Mrs. Lillian Ryan moved into The Villages on October 9, 1967. Her villa was located at 5520 Cribari Circle, B Unit, Building 160. Construction of the village moved along rather quickly and The Villages soon became an active community as more and more families began to move into their new homes.

During 1967, The Villages experienced many firsts. The first resident activity was held on October 27, 1967. A Halloween dinner/dance was held in the Community Hall (Cribari Auditorium) for residents and their guests. This was a way of introducing The Villages as a home and lifestyle to prospective residents. Music was furnished by Ernie Heckscher and his orchestra.

Thursday, November 9, 1967 was the first Fiesta Day held in the Ladies Lounge with eight residents in attendance. The event included a luncheon, followed by

playing the first game of Bingo, which became a Villages' tradition. There were prizes awarded to the winners. The following year, this celebration moved to the patio outside of Cribari Center. Residents were encouraged to come in costume. This event was also an opportunity for guests to tour The Villages.

During this first year, the staff organized events, such as pancake breakfasts and trips to see performances at the Circle Star Theater in San Carlos, just a short drive north of The Villages. The first organized trip for the residents was a tour to the Laguna Art Festival in Laguna Beach, California. The first cultural activity held was a musical concert presented by the Valley of Hearts Delight Recorder Consort, under the direction of Jack C. Russell on December 1, 1967. Approximately 270 people attended. Cookies, punch and coffee were served to the guests after the performance.

In the early part of April 1968, two guest rooms became available for renting in Cribari Center. They are located on the second floor. At a later date two more were added, which made it a total of four rooms. This was a nice amenity for visiting relatives and friends.

To give some reference points for the time frame, this was the same year (1968) that San José got its second TV channel, KGSC (now KICU). (The first channel, KNTV began broadcasting in 1955.) Lyndon B. Johnson was the President of the United States having achieved that position after the assassination of John F. Kennedy in 1963.

The Villages contracted to get their first cable television system with Gould Communication. A closed circuit information channel was set up at that time. Part of is still used today. Following Gould Communications, several firms expanded, operated and maintained the system over the years. Nor Cal was the provider until 2008 when a 15 year contract was signed with Comcast, who provided a much expanded choice of channels. They made internet and telephone service available, as well as television.

Communication is frequently at the top of the list when residents are asked about their concerns. The designated, channel 10's purpose was to notify and keep residents informed of activities and events. It was upgraded in 2008, providing 2 channels; 26 and 27 when Comcast became the television provider.

Another communication tool introduced in 2008 was an instant news messaging service for residents with e-mail. Called The Villages' Fast Lane, it provides information that a resident may have missed in the newspaper and in addition any last minute urgent information.

Keeping up with the times, The Villages developed a web site in 1998. It went through some changes and in 2009, this design greeted visitors.

Our country was in turmoil in 1968, following two more assassinations; Martin Luther King in Tennessee on April 4, 1968 and Robert Kennedy on June 5, 1968 while the latter was campaigning for the Democratic nomination for president of the United States.

Management offered transportation for the residents to the voting polls on November 5, 1968. In subsequent years, The Villages would have their own precincts. The results of the election in 1968 were Richard Nixon as President and Spiro Agnew as Vice president.

At the same time, the United States involvement in the Vietnam War became an area of contention and there were many anti-war demonstrations particularly by the hippies. They came from all over the country to San Francisco on an invitation from a man named Scott McKenzie. By June, with flowers in their hair, the Haight-Ashbury district of San Francisco was awash with *flower power*. This new, formidable group of individuals began questioning the social morals of the older generations.

Here in San José, on October 27, 1968 there was a groundbreaking ceremony for Cribari Knolls. Assemblyman Earle P. Crandall of California's 25th district and special guests Mr. and Mrs. Tony Cribari attended. Within 48 hours of the ceremony, over 25 percent of the homes were sold. By November 1968, sales at The Villages were booming, averaging one a day. The expected completion of Village Cribari was mid-1969. The first year marked the completion of 330 villas.

A new invention appearing in home kitchens at the time was the microwave oven which would have an impact on the designers of the kitchens in the villas being built. This was an opportunity for housewives to create fast food in their own kitchens.

The Villages was the first planned development community with condominiums in San José and Santa Clara County. The original time plan for The Villages' project was five years to completion. In 1979, it had already been 12 years and much more building had still been planned. In actuality it was not completed until 1999.

The land The Villages was built upon was rich in history, particularly viniculture. Wehner, Haentze and Cribari were all winemakers who cultivated this land. When The Villages opened, Tony Cribari was still operating a small portion of his grape orchard. Every fall, for about six weeks, grapes were harvested. When the harvest concluded, there was a grape harvest festival hosted by Tony. This continued until the Cribaris sold the remainder of the winery property to Atkinson-Mackay in 1974.

Local Services

When construction of The Villages began in 1967, there was very little development in the Evergreen section of San José and therefore many residents felt very isolated. It was an excursion traveling to other areas of San José for shopping. Many Villagers moved here from cities where the simple necessities were much closer to their homes.

In response to this need, a transportation system was inaugurated. Management arranged for a regularly scheduled bus that came into The Villages and picked up people in front of Cribari Center. The bus took residents to a shopping center on the corner of White and Aborn Roads and a second one at White and Story Road. The latter had a Safeway grocery store as one of the retail establishments. In January 1970 the bus service was extended to include trips to downtown San José.

January 1973 brought a new service to the residents. A small bus provided by the management of The Villages, with a capacity of eight people provided transportation to some local shopping centers. The bus left from Cribari and Montgomery and went to Eastridge,

Formerly 5¢ and 10¢ store at White and Aborn

the Safeway store, downtown San José, the bus terminal and train station. It ran Monday, Tuesday, Thursday and Friday. Priority use was given to those residents who were non-drivers.

A year later, on a trial basis for two months, a bus left from Cribari Village Center for the Pruneyard Shopping Center in Campbell. The bus was funded by The Pruneyard. It would pick up residents for shopping and lunch at The Pruneyard. Two months later it was cancelled due to scant usage.

Another bus service for The Villages was provided by Santa Clara County Transit starting in July 1975. The Villages was the terminus of a new Santa Clara transit line. It ran weekdays from Cribari Center to Eastridge Shopping Mall and then on to Milpitas. With one transfer, residents could travel to BART in Fremont, downtown San José, Santa Clara Shopping Center, El Paseo de Saratoga, San José State University, San José City College, Alexian Brothers Hospital and the Valley Medical Center all for 25¢ or 10¢ for those handicapped or over 65 years of age.

Free bus passes with residents' photographs were issued in October 1981 on yet another bus. The shopping bus, as it was called, would deliver residents to their doors and the driver would assist in carrying packages into the house. In 1985, the shopping bus was discontinued.

Several banks chose to build branch offices at The Villages. This addition would be another convenience for the Villagers. In October 1968, the Bank of America opened a branch office in a temporary prefabricated building at the back of Cribari Center. The hours were very limited; 11:00 a.m. to 2:00 p.m. Monday through Friday. In 1970, the Bank of America printed special edition checks depicting the Villages' bell logo. The Bank of America broke ground for its new building next to the Villages Plaza in February 1980.

Western Federal Savings and Loan secured Federal Government approval in October 1974 to open a branch office at The Villages.

They opened their temporary location in the administration offices across from the tennis courts, near the sales information center in March 1975. The bank relocated to a new building located on the north east corner of Hounds Estates and Villages Parkway in 1976.

In April 1983, Western Federal was replaced by Downey Savings and Loan. In November 1997, Downey Savings moved into a new building in Villages Plaza and in 2008 it was absorbed by US Bank. After Downey Savings moved, their former building was sold to an orthodontist.

In August 1984, California Federal provided free bus service from Cribari Center to the Friday evening performances of the San José Symphony Orchestra for the 1984-85 season ticket holders.

The San José Post Office opened a sub-station in The Villages in 1968, which is still in service today. The U.S. Postal Service trains the clerks. It is a very efficient service, and though small, it can handle most mailing needs from letters to packages. The convenience of having the sub-station in Cribari Center saves Villagers the need to travel roughly 20 minutes away to the next closest post office.

Medical Facility

Dr. Robert Condie

In early 1968, a medical office facility was established in Cribari Center. The Villages' Medical Center was a fully equipped medical facility with the most modern medical equipment available at the time. The equipment was provided by Atkinson - Mackay. Dr. Robert S. Condie was the physician on staff and Mrs. Shore, RN joined the medical facility a short time later. Prior to its opening, the first professional resident activity of The Villages' Medical team was a house call made by the resident physician on November 12, 1967. The first consultation, by appointment in The Villages' Medical Center was on December 5,

1967. The facility formally opened in January 1968. For a short time, the San José Medical Group ran a free van service from The Villages to its main facility in downtown San José.

Seasonal influenza vaccine was developed in the 40's by the US military and used during World War II. By 1967 it was widely available and recommended for people over 50 years of age. In October 1968, prior to the flu season, influenza vaccine was available at the Villages' Medical Clinic.

Dr. Jackson Flanders joined Dr. Condie at the medical facility in September 1969. This gave the residents additional medical coverage. Dr. Flanders was a resident of Village Cribari.

In March 1971, a full optometry service was opened in the Medical facility. Appointments were available on Thursday afternoons with Drs. Gilmer and Lohr O.D. Dr. Aagesen, a resident of the Villages, also joined the medical group that same year. He was a specialist in diseases of the ear, nose, throat and nasal allergy. In 2002, Dr. Aagesen was honored as the Grand Marshal of The Villages 4th of July parade along with Bertha Seley. They were the surviving original Cribari residents at the time.

After several changes in hours of operation, by June 1971, the clinic extended its hours. It was open 9:00 a.m. to 5:00 p.m. with medical care available 24 hours a day, seven days a week by doctors of The Villages' Medical Group; a professional corporation.

A pharmacy, which was part of the long-range goal of making the Villages a complete community, opened in March of 1968. William Forest, the pharmacist, sold prescription drugs as well as health equipment. The first prescription # 1000 was filled and delivered on March 28, 1968. They offered standard immunizations to the residents. In the beginning, the pharmacy was open Friday mornings, but by 1970, the hours were extended to include afternoon service, 5 days a week. As the use of the pharmacy grew, the inventory expanded to include some non-

William Forest

prescription drugs and medications. When William Forest retired in 1975, Mr.

Ron Keil replaced him. The pharmacy moved to The Villages Plaza and Mr. Keil continued as the pharmacist until Longs Drug Store opened on San Felipe Road and Yerba Buena Road. Mr. Keil closed the pharmacy in the Villages Plaza and worked for Longs until his retirement.

1977 brought another change when some associate doctors resigned, leaving Dr. Condie as the only doctor managing the medical program. By 1979 the number of residents had increased and therefore the need for another doctor. Dr. Lewis W. Berry joined Dr. Condie in the Medical Group that year. Dr. Condie retired from the San José Medical Clinic and from The Villages' staff in 1975. Until finding a replacement, several internists rotated through The Villages.

Santa Teresa Hospital Outpatient Medical Services assumed the management and operation of the center in February 1976. Dr. Condie returned and was once again The Villages' physician. Dr. Paul Pettit joined the staff. A podiatrist, Dr. Leonard Greenwald joined the medical group in February 1977. His office was open one afternoon a week.

A dream of Dr. Condie's came to fruition in June of 1968 when a Villages Medical Center Auxiliary (VMA) was established. The first piece of equipment was a pair of crutches. There was so much excitement that Dr. Condie had a celebration party and said, "We are on our way." Thanks to the foresight of this man, we have the VMA that serves the community in many ways. Donations make it possible to maintain a supply of medical equipment such as wheel chairs, walkers, canes, etc. which the VMA loans out free of charge. They also offer rides to doctors' appointments, convalescent facilities and grocery shopping trips for those who can no longer drive.

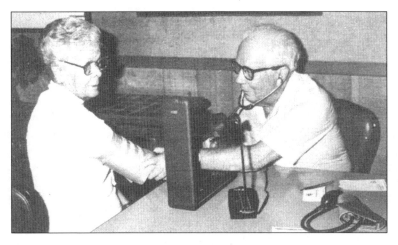

The medical profession has linked many serious diseases; some fatal, to high blood pressure. In April 1983, the VMA started sponsoring weekly professional blood pressure clinics that made it convenient for the residents to keep a close check on their blood pressure without traveling a good distance to their doctor.

Several Automated External Defibrillators (AED) were purchased by The Villages in late 2002. They were placed in strategic locations, such as Cribari Center and the swimming pools. The following January, there were AED training classes offered which were sponsored by the Emergency Preparedness Committee (EPC) and the VMA.

In June 2004, the VMA sponsored the first of what was to be an annual health fair. This provided Villagers with a convenient source of information that would be difficult for the average person to find on their own.

Strong and Company, an Insurance company, opened an office in the Medical facility in March 1968. Three years later in 1971, they moved from that location to the Villages Plaza. The professional center in Cribari continued to grow with the addition of a beauty shop which opened toward the end of 1975.

Dentistry was offered to the residents by Josiah D. Beck D.D.S. in the Professional Center in The Villages starting in 1975.

By 1981, there was a full Medical Staff, which included:

Robert S. Condie, MD   - geriatrics
David Silverstein, MD   - ophthalmology
Mary Pannell, DPM   - podiatry
Walter Aagesen, MD   - specialist in allergy and ear, nose & throat
Joseph Geare, PAC   - physicians assistant who left in May 1981 after one
                            year of service.

Dr. Robert S. Condie retired from the medical facility in April 1982 and was replaced by Dr. Barbara Campbell. She worked at The Villages until June 1988 when she resigned from the medical facility. This forced the closing of The Villages' Branch of the San José Medical Group.

March 1988 - The Villages Medical Center relocated to 2500 Villages Parkway from their earlier location at 5003 Cribari Lane. This location was in the office complex that is now Building C. The services still available were; Dr. Aagesen, ear, nose & throat; David S. Silverstein, ophthalmologist; Rachel Wood D.P.M., podiatrist.

Public Safety

Gatehouse 1975

The main reason given by many residents why they made The Villages their home is the feeling of security. Having an entrance and gate house staffed by security guards around the clock, 365 days per year fulfills this need.

Entrance security was operating as soon as The Villages opened and residents were issued bumper stickers for identification. They were Scotch-lite stickers with the name The Villages and a rendition of the bell logo. Some residents objected to a full bumper sticker, so permission was granted for the use of the bell, alone. These bumper stickers changed every year, which was a big expense. Affixed to the windshield starting in 1990, was a smaller sticker with The Villages logo in blue and white. These were readily visible by the security team at the gate.

The logo that was used was a rendition of the Villages Crest that was designed in 1972 by Hank Volle. The original painting of the logo was green with gold thread highlights. This logo is used for letterheads, identification on The Villages' trucks and other forms of communication.

In 1970, speed limits were set in The Villages. On the Parkway, outside the gate, the speed was 35 miles per hour and once you passed through the gate, the speed was 25 miles per hour.

Remodeling and moving of the Security Plaza further up the Parkway toward The Villages improved traffic flow into The Villages in 1972. It also enabled the security officer on duty to stand outside and talk to visitors without leaving the building site. The left hand lane inbound was for guests and the right hand lane for the residents with the proper identification sticker displayed on the windshield.

The installation of a flagpole and American flag, donated by the High Twelve Club at the Security gate in May 1974, gave the residents and their guests a patriotic feeling when entering The Villages. An American flag has proudly flown there continuously since that time. The Hi Twelve club replaces the flag as needed.

The Security Gate building moved to its permanent location in February 1975. The center strip on Villages Parkway up to Hounds Estate again became the responsibility of The Villages Community Services Department. This made it possible for The Villages to have a permanent Security Office and gate. Prior to this, the center strip was owned by the City of San José.

In January 1980, a station wagon was purchased to replace the patrol truck for the Security Department. It was felt that the station wagon would provide greater transportation flexibility. This made a good vehicle to take residents to airports, medical clinics and hospitals. During the day, its use was a patrol vehicle. Three trucks equipped with bar lights that are used for emergencies, as well as patrolling, eventually replaced it.

There was another reconstruction, as well as a name change to Security Plaza in 1987. A bar code sticker placed on the window of the cars activated the gate electronically beginning in 1999 and went into effect in February 2001.

A big event on the national scene in July 1969 was the successful landing on the moon by a team of astronauts.

Emergency Aid

A ribbon cutting ceremony on June 20, 1980, was held for the opening of Fire Station # 11 located on Villages Parkway just outside the Security Plaza. The fire station, which is part of the San José City Fire Department, was designed as a residential fire station with Spanish motif in order to blend in with the design of

The Villages' architectural style. The station houses an engine company with a daily manning strength of one captain, one fire engineer and two firefighters.

Fire station 2010

The residents in The Villages have come to appreciate the importance of having a fire station in close proximity. Station #11 answers an average of three calls a day and 50 percent of its calls are for aid in The Villages. If the ambulance company is not able to respond quickly, the firefighters call on Station #31, which is located on Ruby Avenue, for their transport vehicle.

In addition to the protection of the fire department, a very vital committee was formed in December 1981, called the Emergency Preparedness Committee (EPC). The EPC's purpose is "to inform the Villages' residents of ways and means to prepare for disaster situations and, in the event of a disaster, to coordinate the operation and use of critical resources to maintain the maximum resident support to preserve life and property." EPC has organized The Villages to be prepared. Each of the 12 districts (Villages) is divided into smaller sectors. These sectors have a leader and several assistants whose purpose is to assist their neighbors when emergencies arise. EPC is so well organized; some outside groups have visited to observe how it is accomplished. It is this group that initiated the Vial of Life at The Villages, which is a small container (vial) that is placed in the refrigerator with all the necessary information that would be needed in an emergency situation; such as contact people, drug information, physical limitations, etc. The fire department and ambulance companies know about the vial and its location.

In July 1995, a fire occurred in The Villages. It burned the carport roofs in the Cribari Center parking lot. The blaze started from something burning underneath the hood of one of the cars. The flames leapt from vehicle to vehicle, resulting in total destruction of five resident-owned vehicles. The roof and any personal property that was stored in the wooden cabinets were lost. The laundry room in the carport also sustained damage. Fortunately, there were no injuries. The fire originated with an electrical short and arcing. There was a second fire in the golf cart area in Cribari Hills in November 1997.

A major residential fire in The Villages for the first time in 41 years occurred May 18, 2008. A four alarm fire with 25 fire engines and 100 firefighters responded to a fire which was in a condominium on Cribari Vale. The fire damaged eight units in one building with four totally destroyed. One man died in the inferno. It was the first time in the history of The Villages that fire totally destroyed some residential property.

Four neighboring condominiums also sustained significant damage. EPC mobilized quickly and was instrumental in assisting displaced residents. Besides EPC, many residents assisted by going from door to door to check on other neighbors. The outpouring of love was a testimony to the people in The Villages.

Hermosa Village was the scene for a fire in 2009. It occurred in a newly purchased condominium prior to the residents taking occupancy. There was some interior damage.

Another fire in 2010 in Village del Lago resulted in a second death. The fire was contained to the bedroom.

Awards

The Villages received the Award of Distinction by the national publication, *The Builder Magazine* in 1968. The award was presented to C. Robert Moon, Sales

Director of the Villages, at a ceremony during the annual convention of the National Home Builders Association. The honor was "In recognition of excellence of design and construction".

The Villages received another award when it was designated the Outstanding Adult Community in Northern California for 1976 by the Construction Council of California and the Bay Area Building Reporter. There were 30 communities vying for this distinction.

More recognition for The Villages was received in 1990 and 1992. In the publication, *New Choices for Retirement Living* The Villages was listed as one of the twenty top retirement communities. *Retirement Living: a guide to the best residences in Northern California* (1990) was another publication that listed the Villages. Then two years later, The Villages earned the distinction of a listing in *The 99 Best Residential & Recreational Communities in America*.

Always mindful of conservation, in June 1994, The Villages received an award for its water conservation efforts.

Dining

The Terrace Room, the first restaurant, had its preview opening on Tuesday, January 2, 1968 for the Villages' personnel. There were four customers for lunch that ran up a total tab of $7.16. The Terrace Room officially opened for residents on Wednesday, January 3, 1968 at 11:00 a.m. Lunch was served between 11:00 a.m. and 2:00 p.m. The first day there were 16 customers. A total of $13.59 was collected. For the first year or two, the staff also did double duty as the servers in the restaurant.

The Terrace Room was located in Cribari Center between the men's and ladies' lounges according to the original plan of the center. There was a kitchen downstairs, so all the food could be prepared on the premises. The restaurant was small, but intimate. In April, the hours were extended to include dinner on Friday evenings. In November of the same year, the restaurant opened for breakfast and lunch seven days a week and dinner on selective evenings.

With a community that was steadily growing, the restaurant struggled to keep up with the desires of the residents as well as trying to make the operation cost effective. As a result, over the years, this service frequently changed in location as well as hours of operation.

Events, such as potluck dinners, bridge games, dominoes and pocket billiards as well as Spaghetti feeds followed by Bingo were scheduled commencing in January of the first year. Due to the larger attendance, they were held in Cribari Auditorium. These functions were well attended and provided opportunities for new residents to meet other people. In 1970, a special menu was introduced with live Maine lobster served every Saturday and Sunday in the Terrace Room.

A fire in the Terrace room kitchen occurred in January 1972, which necessitated closing the facility during the repairs, but the auditorium remained open for events. In the early part of 1975 and again in 1981, the Terrace Room underwent some remodeling.

The Terrace Room discontinued lunch service when the popular Pro-shop Grille opened in March of 1978. The residents gave it the official name of The Grille. In May 1981, The Terrace Room closed except for group and banquet functions and The Grille extended its hours and opened for din-

ner. It remained open until October 1995, when it was demolished in preparation for the new clubhouse. During the interim period, The Terrace Room served breakfast and lunch to accommodate the services that The Grille had offered.

VILLAGES FOOD SERVICE

TERRACE ROOM

Dinner is served in the Terrace Room from 5 until 9 p.m., Wednesday through Saturday and from 5 until 8 p.m. on Sunday. Breakfast is served in the Terrace Room on Sunday from 9 a.m. until 12 noon. Reservations will be accepted for parties of five or more. Call the Terrace Room, Wednesday through Sunday after 4 p.m., 274-2255.

TERRACE ROOM MENU

The following are regular menu items:
New York Strip Steak........$9.95
Slimliner...................$5.95
New York Steak & Prawns.....$8.95
Louisiana Prawns............$7.95
Sea Scallops................$7.50
Fresh Filet of Sole.........$7.50

— TERRACE ROOM SPECIALS —

Friday, December 3:
Rock Cornish Game Hens with Rice Stuffing and Mushroom Sauce, $7.95

Saturday, December 4:
Beef Burgundy with Rice Pilaf, $6.95

Sunday, December 5:
Roast Cross Rib of Beef, $7.95

Wednesday, December 8:
Roast Turkey with Dressing, Mashed Potatoes, Vegetable, $6.95

Thursday, December 9:
Baked Ham with Raisin Sauce, $6.95

Friday, December 10:
Veal Cordon Bleu, $7.95

Saturday, December 11:
Prime Rib of Beef (extra cut) $10.95

Sunday, December 12:
Scampi, Complete Dinner, $8.95

GRILLE

The Grille is open daily from 7 a.m. until 5 p.m., rain or shine!

Breakfast   7 a.m. - 2 p.m.
Lunch   11 a.m. - 2:30 p.m.
Cold Food   2 p.m. - 5 p.m.

GRILLE SPECIALS

Monday, December 6:
Cream Cheese, Alfalfa Sprouts & Bacon Sandwich, $3.50

Tuesday, December 7:
Chili Burger, $3.50

Wednesday, December 8:
Ham & Cheese Omelette, $3.50

Thursday, December 9:
Turkey with Bacon Sandwich, $3.50

Friday, December 10:
Fish & Chips, $4.50

A daily special is served at The Grille, Monday through Friday. The price includes entree, dessert and beverage. In addition, a full menu is available.

MENU PLANNING

To assist you in your menu planning for functions at The Villages, the following schedule is available:

Wednesday & Friday, 10 a.m. until 12 noon, or by appointment.

To contact Jenny's Restaurant, call 274-6711.

December 1982

As a result of a committee study, in October 1982, an outside company, owned by Mr. and Mrs. Chu was chosen to provide the food service. Both The Grille and The Terrace Room began serving meals on a regular basis. In 1983, the restaurant was renamed Jenny's Restaurant.

Outsourcing of the operation of the restaurant was concluded in 1986, at which time the facility was refurbished and re-opened, with our own staff, in November of that same year. A community wide contest resulted in the return to the name of The Terrace Room. At this time it was relocated, up a few steps into the larger room of the Cribari complex (currently called the Men's lounge).

After the Clubhouse was built in June 1998, the earlier location of the Terrace Room was renovated and renamed The Terrace Lounge. Its purpose became a drop-in lounge with a large television and access to the kitchen.

The other two rooms in that wing became the Men's and Ladies' lounges and are the location of choice for playing games such as bridge, dominoes and Mah Jongg along with a variety of other table-top games.

Villages' Sports

The Villages Golf and Country Club golf course was designed by Robert Muir Graves, a well-known golf course architect. He flew in to San José Airport in 1967 with a large bag filled with cans of spray paint in a variety of colors. After arriving at The Villages, he proceeded to walk the proposed course, spraying different colors of paint on the site in order to identify the placement of various aspects of the course.

The long-awaited opening of the golf course became a reality on March 29, 1968. The first nine holes were officially opened when Mr. Jack C. Mackay teed off by hitting a gold ball. The first foursome was chosen by a drawing and the lucky winners were Mr. and Mrs. Gustav R. Weinkauf (Elsa), Mrs. Mabel Du-Bois and Mr. Paul J. Todsen. The course was played twice in order to complete 18 holes.

Vice-mayor Norman Mineta was at The Villages to see the beginning earth moving for the second 9 holes for the golf course in April 1969. The full 18 hole course was completed and opened in July 1970.

Two big tournaments of note in 1972 were the 36[h] Masters played in Augusta, Georgia with Jack Nicklaus, the winner and the first North-South men's tournament and invitational played at The Villages in San José, California. Village Cribari was divided in two sections; north and south. The golfers in Montgomery were on the south team. They competed against each other in the full spirit of a war battle; secret meetings to plan strategy, players ranked e.g., commander, colonel, etc. The reenactments added to the spirit of the game.

Development of the first phase of the driving range began in November 1973 and opened in May of 1974. Guy F. Atkinson offered The Villages Golf and Country Club the opportunity to purchase the driving range for $200,000 in August of 1985. This was approved by the Board of Directors in September.

A Pro-shop was built and dedicated on March 23, 1978.

With a first class golf course at The Villages, several golf clubs formed fulfilling different needs. There is the Men's Club who plays the full 18 holes, the Men's Long Nine-Hole and the Ironmen who play the short nine course. The women also have three groups: the Eighteen Hole Belles, the Swingers, who play the long nine and the Shonis, who play the short nine. All of these groups have their specified day for play. They also sponsor invitationals and many other social events. In 2010, the name of the short nine course was changed to the Par 3 course.

There are many people at The Villages who do not play golf, but appreciate the beauty that the rolling greens and trees bring to the community. The paths on the golf course also afford a beautiful walk when golf is not in progress.

A physically active community would not be complete without some tennis courts. The decision to build some courts was made in 1969 with construction beginning in 1970. The original two courts were built by Atkinson/ Mackay. In

addition to the tennis courts were shuffle board courts, archery courts and horseshoe pits. The latter were located in the recreational area near the Pro Shop, next to the first green of the golf course.

The long-awaited opening of the tennis courts occurred in June, 1970. The tennis players formed teams in order to compete in interclub tournaments. Today, some of the players choose to play in United States Tennis Association (U.S.T.A) tournaments. To participate in U.S.T.A. tournaments, the players must be ranked and then the match is between players with the same ranking.

Expansion with the addition of two more courts occurred in 1978. The Villages' tennis teams were ready to practice for Wimbledon in 1978, after watching Björn Borg of Sweden win the men's singles and Martina Navratilova of the United States win the women's singles.

In order to facilitate watching the tennis competitions at The Villages, a tennis viewing stand was built and dedicated in June 1997. Due to the popularity of tennis, in the summer of 1998, two additional tennis courts were constructed. The new courts were built with money from donations by the Tennis Club.

Looking back, as long ago as 5000 BC, the Egyptians played a form of Bocce with polished rocks. From Egypt the game made its way to Greece about 800 B.C. The Romans learned the game from the Greeks and it developed into the game that we know today which is played at The Villages. In the early years, the Romans used coconuts that were brought back from Africa and they later carved balls out of olive wood. The early participants of Bocce including the Greek physician Hippocrates and physician/ astronomer Galileo noted that, "the game's athleticism and spirit of competition rejuvenates the body".

During the earlier years of The Villages, Bocce was played by small groups of friends on the lawns in various locations around the community. Two official Bocce courts became a reality in November 2002. Gazebo Park was chosen as the ideal location. To complete the area, scoreboards, a storage cabinet and tables were added. The Bocce Club was formed and teams organized for competitive play. A very popular event is the Friday evening Bocce Bash.

In January 1975, an exercise room, located in Building C, opened for the use of the residents. There were separate hours for men and women. Men had the use of the room until 10:30 a.m., women from 10:30 a.m. until 2:00 p.m. After 2:00 p.m. it was on a first-come, first-served basis. Later, in 1999 it expanded to a larger room in Montgomery Center. With the expansion,  more equipment was added. The fitness center has undergone several improvements over the years.

In addition to the center itself and what it offers, there are many fitness programs offered at The Villages, such as; Yoga, balance and walking classes, Tai Chi, Jazzercise, line dancing, a Parkinson's support group and more.

A group of Villagers formed a Croquet group in July 1999. True to the traditions of croquet, they donned their white shirts and slacks and gathered on the Village Green to enjoy the fellowship and camaraderie of the game. (The Village Green is an area north of The Villages Parkway, near the Security Plaza at the entrance to The Villages.)

There is an active and very competitive table tennis group that meets to play several times a week in the Club Room. They hold competitions among themselves and meet competitively with other communities, such as Rossmoor.

Another amenity at The Villages is a Billiard Room. There are three games that are played in the Billiard Room. The first and most popular is the game of Pool that has many variations. There are two pool tables for this purpose. Second to that in popularity is the game of Snooker which is a traditional English game that has its own table. In addition, there is also the game of Billiards. It is played on a table without any pockets. It is frequently known as Three Cushion Billiards or No pocket Billiards.

The players do not have an official club. There are some players assigned to look after the facility, but the games are not organized. The cues and balls are provided and keyed access to the room allows residents to play at their convenience. Many of the Pool and Snooker players have their own cues, which are placed in a special cabinet when leaving the room. Some of the players are residents using the facility primarily to entertain guests.

The Hiking Club, as well as energetic Villagers, benefit from the 546 acres of undeveloped hill land that was deeded to The Villages Golf and Country Club, on January 1, 1978 by Atkinson-Mackay. Zoned as a recreational area, it provides open space and maintains the natural landscape as a background to The Villages' community.

Originally the hill land was leased for cattle grazing. The cattle kept the grass short and therefore minimized fire danger. Wild game abounds in this area. Deer, elk, wild pigs, quail, buzzards, hawks, golden eagles and turkeys have all been sighted.

Over the years, many trails have been developed in the hills, one of which was dedicated to Joe Marsh, a horticulturalist who lead informative excursions identifying wildflowers, etc. for his fellow hikers.

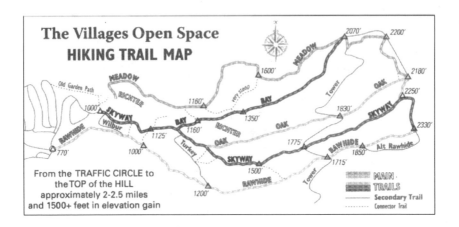

The Villages Open Space
HIKING TRAIL MAP

From the TRAFFIC CIRCLE to
the TOP of the HILL
approximately 2-2.5 miles
and 1500+ feet in elevation gain

Due to this natural expanse of space, it was only natural that a Hiking Club formed. They meet once a week trekking to various locations both within The Villages, as well as to other points of interest off site.

Another use of the hill lands is for riding horses. A number of people moved to The Villages, having had a horse at their former home. A proposed plan for a horse stable was approved by the San José City Council and the construction began in March 1972. It opened for their new residents (horses) in May of that same year in the area that is now Village Highland. This made it more convenient for the equestrians than finding a stable outside The Villages to board their horses.

Across the country, two other horses, Riva Ridge and Secretariat were stabled in Kentucky. Riva Ridge won the Kentucky Derby in 1972; Secretariat was the Triple Crown winner in 1973.

In September 1978, the stable was moved to its permanent location up the hill beyond Foothill Center. The stable was cut in half, lengthwise and trailered from Village Highland to the present location. Besides the stable, there is also a ring for training and exercising the horses and adequate space to park the horse trailers. There are a total of 11 stalls and in 2010, they were all occupied. The food, alfalfa and orchard grass is hauled to the site by a truck.

Some equestrians take their horses to riding events that are held at various sites, such as Calaro, Quicksilver and the Santa Clara Horseman's Headquarters. Here at home, there are approximately 500 acres with multiple wide trails and many other small trails for the equestrians' use.

Full body exercise is the goal of active people. Swimming fulfills that goal. A total of four pools are located in The Villages. Every summer, water aerobics classes are offered. From the time the pools are opened at 6 a.m. until they close at 10 p.m. in the evening, rain or shine, residents can be seen doing laps for exercise or using the spas for therapy.

Cribari swimming pool opened September 16, 1968. It was officially opened by Charles W. Williams, Vice President of The Villages Board of Directors. To help with the cost of heating water, solar panels were installed in 2002.

Dippy Dolphins were inaugurated in the early days of The Villages because of the lovely swimming pools in the community. Dippy Dolphins, a fun loving and love to swim group meet on a regular basis at Montgomery pool. The choice of the name is so appropriate, as the dolphin is such a friendly and playful mammal, as well as being a magnificent swimmer. Because the purpose of the group was to have fun and good times, they added the descriptive title of Dippy.

Montgomery Pool was the second pool built, in 1974. There is a beautiful view of this pool from the Montgomery clubhouse.

The Vineyard swimming pool opened in October 1980.

The Villages' swimmers were ready to make use of this new facility after being inspired by the summer Olympics that were held in Moscow that summer.

Foothill pool opened in April 2000. The structure of this pool is quite different from the other three. It was designed as a lap pool. Therefore the depth is constant for the whole length of the pool.

There are also those people who love the fresh air and the sounds of birds in the trees and the beautiful scenery as they utilize the miles of walking paths throughout The Villages. These paths were part of the community's master plan when each village was built.

Religious Services

In all religious faiths, worshipping with fellow believers gives people strength and encouragement, especially in times of need. Various religious communities hold regularly scheduled services at The Villages.

The first church service at The Villages was held Sunday, September 22, 1968 in Cribari Auditorium. The non-denominational Protestant service was conducted by Rev. E.V. Steele, a former missionary and resident of The Villages. A part-time pastor for the chapel started serving the congregation on January 23, 1972. In 1981, the Chapel leased some office space from The Villages in Building D. In the beginning, the Chapel shared the use of the office with an insurance representative of Rollins Burdick Hunter, who used the space on Thursdays.

The first Catholic mass was held on November 17, 1969 in Cribari Auditorium. Most Rev. Msgr. James F. Maher, pastor of Holy Trinity Church, conducted the mass. In April 1998, a new sanctuary, St. Francis of Assisi was built and dedicated a short distance away on San Felipe Road. Two masses continue to be held at The Villages on a regular basis.

Episcopal Services are held weekly at Montgomery Center. The parent church for this congregation is St. Phillips on Alum Rock Avenue in San José. St. Phillips, at The Villages, held its first service in 1974.

A group from the Christian community meets for a Bible study called, Search the Scriptures. Originally, with a group of five, they met in homes. As the group grew, they moved to the Library and ultimately to one of the community centers. With a leader, who challenges them to grow on a daily basis, they delve into the Bible to study God's word.

The Jewish Community organized their group in January 1979. The High Holy Day services of Rosh Hashanah and Yom Kippur were held at The Villages starting in 2002. Sabbath services are held monthly, followed by a program. In the spring, a Seder dinner is held at the Clubhouse. Chanukah is celebrated with a dinner followed by a service.

Brandeis National Committee Club is a philanthropic group that raises money for scholarships and research for Brandeis University in Massachusetts. The Santa Clara

Valley Chapter, of which Villagers are members, has small interest groups among which are study groups, currents events, hand arts and more.

Hadassah is a Women's Zionist Organization of America who raises money for Israel, specifically hospitals and research. The local group in The Villages meets regularly for socializing and planning events, one of which is the popular village-wide game day held twice a year.

Music

The Villages has some very musically gifted people in its midst. Sharing these gifts and their love of music led these individuals to form groups for their particular interest.

The first of the musical groups to organize was those who played musical instruments. In March 1977, the sounds of music could be heard as the practice sessions began for a concert band. The Villages has a full concert band that gives much anticipated performances for the enjoyment of their fellow Villagers and guests.

Until 2009, there was also a Swing Band that played for social dances and other venues. After performing for many years, the group disbanded.

Marshall Dahneke, a

former director of The Villages concert band, composed a rhapsody entitled *Cribari Vale*. It was performed for the first time on March 17, 1992.

In February 1978, The Villages Choraliers was formed. This was a chorus that became The Village Voices. The Voices practice regularly in preparation for two performances a year which they give for the enjoyment of the residents and friends. They are frequently in concert with the Villages' band. They also perform at the Veterans' Day program on November 11 and when requested at special events.

A handbell group, The Villages Handbell Ensemble was formed in 1996. With their gloves and bells set out in front of them, they perform concerts in conjunction with the concert band.

A subset of the group, The Harmony Bells performs outside of The Villages at rest homes, community centers and parties. Along with the Voices and The Villages Band, they are a wonderful addition to the Veterans' Day program.

Since about 1989, a piano club has performed for the enjoyment of the Villagers. They are a group of people who are interested in a broad range of music, from classical to jazz. The group is comprised of amateurs as well as those who are close to professional. They meet to share their love of the piano and in the process motivate and inspire each other. Once a year, the pianists give a group recital for The Villages. They are part of the Music Society and help to sponsor their activities. They gave a benefit concert in 2010, for the purpose of the procurement of a grand piano for The Villages.

An Opera Lovers group was formed to bring opera to The Villages via DVDs. Meeting once a month this group views various well-known operas and investigates little known operas. They promote San José Opera, as well as supporting them with donations.

Entertainment

A smile always came to everyone's face when the Easter Bunny visited The Villages each spring and could be seen hiding eggs in the shrubbery around Cribari Center. At other times of the year, the only rabbits visible were the large jack rabbits who also call The Villages their home. This annual event which began in 1969 brought many grandchildren to The Villages.

Little girls in their Easter finery and pretty bonnets and little boys, all with baskets in their small hands hunted for the golden egg and the other goodies that were hidden. Besides the egg hunt, there was some child oriented entertainment and of course, refreshments. Each child went home with an Easter basket full of delights.

The Activities Committee who sponsored this event had as much fun as the children. Baskets were filled the day before, eggs were hidden and there were always some adult-sized bunnies hopping around.

Riding down from the Ponderosa to The Villages on Saturday, May 31, 1969 was Ben Cartwright alias Lorne Greene (of the TV program *Bonanza* fame) to help entertain those attending the Fiesta Grand Ball in Cribari Center.

The ball drew over one hundred guests from the Santa Clara Valley and the Peninsula. Also attending the ball were Mayor and Mrs. Ron James. Mr. Green was on stage to give a brief presentation before the ball began and led the Grand March during the ball. Not much dancing was done by Mr. Greene as everyone wanted to meet him personally.

The following day the television star acted as Grand Marshall in the Fiesta de Las Roses Parade along the Alameda. The parade originated in 1896 as the Carnival of Roses. In 1926, Cora Older chaired the committee for the organization of the Fiesta. She changed the name to the Fiesta de Las Roses. According to the newspapers, it rivaled the Tournament of Roses Parade held in Pasadena every New Years Day.

Another name change and new logo in 1969 is pictured here. The parade honored the rich history of San José. The Villages had a float in the parade in 1969. The design of The Villages' float, in keeping with the Heritage theme of the parade was constructed by Director Bob Frost and his art class members. Atkinson-Mackay supplied the materials. A revival of the Fiesta from the late 1920's and 1930's was combined with the celebration of the California Bicentennial 1769-1969. The parade and ball climaxed a week of activities that included a rodeo, a golf tournament, concerts, a wine festival, queen contest and several other sports events.

"Happy New Year" could be heard echoing around The Villages in 1969 and every year since, as friends gathered to celebrate at one of the gala New Years Eve parties. The first year the event was held in Cribari Center and the popularity of that first New Years celebration was evident as the years went by. After the Clubhouse was built, an elegant, formal dinner dance in the Clubhouse was added. At the same time was a less formal party with dinner and dancing was held in Cribari Auditorium. An Early Bird dinner at the Café always drew a large group of Villagers and their guests.

Movies came to The Villages in 1970. The theater was in Cribari Center. The closest commercial movie theater was in downtown San José. For the Cribari Theater, there was a charge to the residents of 65¢ to defray the cost of renting the film. In a theater outside The Villages, in 1970, the ticket price averaged $1.55. Having the film shown in the community, gave residents a chance to see many new movies including those that were nominated for the Academy Awards. In 1970 the best picture Oscar went to the film *Patton*.

Village Olivas initiated a monthly dinner club in October 1995. This was an opportunity for Olivas' residents to become acquainted with each other in a relaxed setting. It became such a popular event that the rest of the villages started their own dinner clubs.

From time to time, notable political figures have been guests at The Villages. One of the early guests was Nancy Reagan in March 1970. Ronald Reagan was Governor of California from 1967-1975. The San José Republican Women hosted the event that was held at The Villages.

Gathering Places

To further enjoy the beautiful rolling hills and spacious outdoors, two picnic areas were built in the open area along the hiking trails. The first one was planned by the Villages' Management in 1970. They hosted a work party and picnic for the residents who werc interested in developing an area for this use. The Villages' Hiking Club cleared a second area 10 years later and it became the Bay Tree Picnic Area.

The new picnic grove was completed in November 1986 and dedicated in April 1987 to Andrew Fisher; the founder of the hiking club.

In addition, there is a small table and bench at the summit of the trails that hikers use to pause and reflect on the beauty of our hills.

Along Villages Parkway, nestled in a grove of trees is Gazebo Park. Gazebo Park was officially named in June 1979 after a charming gazebo was added to the area. The planting of trees and shrubs at the park was a community project. The various clubs and organizations were asked to contribute to the purchase of the many trees that were in the proposed plan. The Rotary Club of San José did the actual planting and provided additional barbeque grills and also constructed portable picnic tables. The area became a mini park for group picnics and gatherings, as well as family events.

In the summer of 1992, the gazebo was replaced with a sturdier structure. The original gazebo had been a prop from a wedding. The new one was 15 feet in diameter and built from a kit made in Oregon.

The long tables were replaced in 2010 with round tables that seat six people, complete with umbrellas that provide some shade. The gazebo was painted and the grounds leveled.

Besides the Cribari Center and the Clubhouse, The Villages has three smaller community centers. Each of these centers is equipped with a meeting room, full kitchen, a swimming pool and spa.

One is located in the second village built, Village Montgomery. Montgomery Center opened June 22, 1974. It was the first of these facilities built to serve the needs of a group-gathering place, and is located on Wehner Way. The large meeting room with a capacity of 53 people has an attached kitchen; complete with a stove, oven, refrigerator and sink. There is a gas fireplace in the meeting room which lends ambiance to a gathering. In August of that year Montgomery Center was deeded to The Villages Golf and Country Club by the developers, Atkinson-Mackay.

In October 1980, the second social center and swimming pool/ spa opened by the 13th tee. Vineyard Center is a little larger than Montgomery Center and can accommodate 70 people with the same amenities.

Foothill Center, the third of the community centers, opened in August 1999. This facility is located at a higher elevation than the other two and has a beautiful view of the surrounding hills from the pool/ spa area. It is able to accommodate 125 people for a meeting. If food tables are used it can accommodate 100. An added asset at Foothill Center is a barbeque. These centers are in use on a regular basis for meetings, community social functions and private parties.

Celebrations

Ever patriotic, with American flags proudly flying from the homes, The Villages was ready to celebrate the 4th of July with an old-fashioned event. Starting in 1970 a parade with decorated carts, game booths, food and uplifting band music entertained the Villagers and their guests.

Following the parade, there was a barbeque, as well as games for the children. The three-legged race always promoted considerable laughter as the children struggled to reach the finish line. Lt. Gov. Ed Reinecke was the guest speaker that first year.

Water balloon toss

The Villages continued to celebrate with this wonderful event on our nation's Independence Day. Different themes over the years encouraged the residents to put on their creative hats, decorate golf carts and don elaborate costumes.

In 1976, The Villages celebrated the bicentennial of the United States (1776 - 1976). It was a grand parade that year with over 60 floats com-memorating this historical event. The flag bearer was mounted on a fine horse and to make this picture perfect, George Washington ap-peared on a white horse.

The parade's theme in 1984 was Olympiad at The Villages. The Villages' Sons in Retirement (SIR) took the grand prize. The Villages Amateur Theater won the best group entry. From July 28 through August 12, the world Olympics, of-ficially known as the XXIII Olympiad took place in Los Angeles, California, with Carl Lewis bringing home four gold medals for the United States in the 100m, 200m, 4x100m relay and the long jump.

An annual event held in June since 1970, is a pancake breakfast hosted by the Hi-Twelve Club. For many people it has become a yearly tradition to watch these dedicated men flip pancakes on the griddle and serve them steaming hot with all the accoutrements. Families make this a special time together and the grandchildren love the pancakes.

Growth and Development

Since March 1970 there has been an exclusive telephone directory for the use of the residents. In 1971, the directory was printed in color with photographs of the Villagers. As the number of residents increased, due to space restrictions, the photographs were eliminated. An updated directory is published yearly, with an ever changing front cover portraying scenes of The Villages.

As more and more Villagers bought golf carts it became necessary to have a golf cart parking facility. In 1971 this became a reality in the west Cribari parking lot. A second area was later added in the east parking lot.

While Atkinson-Mackay was focused on the design and construction of the villas and roads in Montgomery Village, major technological changes were taking place in the world. The microprocessor was introduced which was the foundation for all computers. The Villages business office would not become computerized until 1981.

CAT or CT (Computed Tomography) scanning was also introduced that same year. This technology greatly benefits people of all ages in diagnostic treatment of illnesses. It was the most important medical breakthrough since the x-ray.

In 1971, the Villages Board presented a proposal to the Planning Commission and the San José City Council for the construction of a grocery store outside The Villages. One week later, a report by Thomas Henderson, board president at the time, confirmed that the Planning Commission approved the plan, designed by Atkinson - Mackay. After discussion, the Board made the decision to postpone the construction until the population of the Villages was larger. There just weren't enough people to support the store. The proposal was withdrawn from the Planning Commission's agenda for the time being.

The following month a second proposal came before the Club Board for a grocery store within The Villages. There was opposition from the eight villas in Village Cribari that were within 200 feet of the proposed location. Finally, after considering many alternatives, the decision was made to utilize Mr. Nelson's former office for the small grocery store. The location was adjacent to the Bank of America in Cribari Center in what is now the Library. On February 22, 1971, The Villages' Board approved the plan to establish a mini market. The market officially opened for business on Tuesday, June 29, 1971. The hours of operation were 9:30 a.m. until 7:00 p.m.

Villager advertisement July 1971

Mr. and Mrs. Mulberry, who were residents of The Villages at the time, were the proprietors of the shop. They also owned a small grocery store in Santa Clara named the Orchard Market. Mr. Mulberry continued to run the Santa Clara store, while Mrs. Mulberry ran the store at The

Villages. The market was carpeted and draped and contained a set of refrigerators, some shelving and a desk. A beginning inventory of 70 or 80 grocery items, some frozen foods, dairy products and bakery goods were available. Also stocked were pet foods, insecticides, periodicals and other miscellaneous supplies.

Orders for grocery items, including meat, that were not stocked in the store, would be placed through Mrs. Mulberry at the convenience store and then delivered by Mr. Mulberry from his Santa Clara market. Deliveries were made each afternoon in Mr. Mulberry's station wagon. Other deliveries included the baked goods, via a bakery wagon and soft drinks delivered once a week.

In March of 1972, Franklin Mulberry sold his Orchard Market in Santa Clara. This enabled him to devote full time to The Villages' Store. The sale did not affect the ordering of the fresh meat and fish. By this time The Villages' store had over 3,000 items in stock.

The Villages' store changed hands in April 1978, when Mr. and Mrs. Mulberry, after seven years of managing the store, retired and moved to Texas. The new management team was Iris and Richard Litrell. In June, after only a couple months, the grocery store management changed again. Lee Benedict became the new manager. In 1981, a grocery store opened in The Villages Plaza, outside the front gate. The Grocery Store in Cribari Center closed its doors the end of March 1981 after many successful years of service to The Villages.

The Villages was growing and by the end of 1971, there was a total population of 947 people living in the community. Changes also took place with The Villages' Board of Directors when it increased in number from five members to seven members.

Activity wise, it was an active year with the ever-popular annual Easter Egg Hunt, the Boosters' Christmas party program, a Halloween party, the May Day picnic, the 4th of July celebration and a spring fling (a social dance and dinner). Social dances have continued to be well attended throughout the years.

Bingo always sustains its popularity. It began as a weekly afternoon game, sponsored by the Activities Committee. After the completion of the Clubhouse, the Clubhouse Committee provided a second opportunity to play Bingo. This event is held bi-monthly, complete with a buffet dinner.

1972 dawned with great expectations for the growth and development of The Villages. The week ending on February 20, 1972, sales set an all-time high. In March 1972, Ray Atkinson replaced Mr. Henderson as General Manager of Atkinson-Mackay at The Villages. Besides this growth of new homes, resulting in new residents, a new education opportunity occurred with the San José Metropolitan Adult Education offering some classes at The Villages.

On the national scene, there was also a change in leadership as Richard Nixon with a new running mate, Spiro Agnew, were victorious in the November election of 1972, which would begin his second term as President of the United States. Spiro Agnew served as his vice-president until October 1974 when he resigned due to a financial scandal and Gerald Ford became the new vice-president. Less than two years later, on August 9, 1974, Richard Nixon resigned from the presidency as a result of the Watergate Scandal. Gerald Ford became the 38th President of the United States. Nelson Rockefeller was chosen to be his Vice President. Note of interest, Gerald Ford was the only president and vice-president not elected into the office.

Each fall in the early years of The Villages' development, there was a Fall Reception with wine and cheese that was sponsored by the management, primarily to welcome new residents and give them a chance to meet other Villagers and become familiar with the varied activities available. Current with the era, women were seen in long dresses and men in suit jackets. Live music set a festive mood for the affair.

For the first time in March 1972, the latest edition of the *San José Evening News* was delivered to The Villages' residents.

July 1973, Singer Homes received city approval for a new street connecting their nearby subdivision, Hounds Estate to Villages Parkway. Villages Parkway is a publicly owned city street from San Felipe Road up to the entrance gate to The Villages.

More changes were occurring, when in October of that same year there was a proposed plan to extend Tully Road through The Villages property. Tully Road would have looped around, crossing Yerba Buena, coming into The Villages, forming a U shape and continuing to San Felipe Road. The proposal was removed from the Evergreen Plan by unanimous vote of the San José City Council after Mr. James F. San Sabastian, (Property Manager for Atkinson-Mackay), sent a letter to Mayor Norman Mineta, promising to cut the density of The Villages from 5,400 villas to 3,000 villas if Tully Road terminated at Yerba Buena. The residents of The Villages were very pleased with the decision for two reasons; 1) they did not want this major road coming through the property and 2) the density of The Villages would be less.

Pacific Gas and Electric announced an energy crisis in January of 1974. In response to the rising cost of electricity, Mr. Nelson published a memo in The Villager newspaper requesting that residents set their thermostats at 68 degrees during the day and lower at night. He also suggested that the gas fireplaces be turned off at night and when not needed.

The primary cause of this crisis was the Arab Oil Embargo, which contributed to a worldwide oil shortage that began on October 17, 1973. Oil prices skyrocketed, as did the prices of other fuels and electricity. There was a rationing of gas in many countries including the United States. Gas procurement regulations were put into effect. Drivers of vehicles with odd-numbered license plates were allowed to purchase gasoline for their cars on Monday, Wednesday and Friday, while drivers of even-numbered license plates were allowed to purchase fuel on Tuesday, Thursday and Saturday. There was a minimum purchase of 6 gallons and a maximum purchase of 15 gallons of gasoline. Drivers could not have more than one quarter of a tank of gasoline when the purchase was made. This resulted in extremely long lines at the gasoline pumps. The embargo was lifted in March 1974, but the effects of the energy crisis lingered throughout the seventies.

In June, 1976, Atkinson-Mackay sold part of The Villages project to Terra California making them the new developers along with Atkinson - Mackay. Ray Atkinson, Director of The Villages Association, The Villages Community Services Corporation and The Villages Golf and Country Club was elected Senior Vice-president of the Guy F. Atkinson Company.

In the center of The Villages, regally stands the Wehner Mansion that was mentioned earlier in the book. In May of 1978, it was chosen for the San José Symphony Auxiliary's Decorators Showcase, which was a yearly event. The five dollar admission fee went to benefit the San José Symphony. Local interior designers decorated the rooms in a variety of styles. The mansion was again, for a short period of time, restored to its original elegance.

In 1986 there was a proposal by UDC to renovate the mansion and bring it up to current building codes with the thought of using it as an added facility for The Villages. The residents would be assessed a small amount for this purpose. It was never realized, as the future Clubhouse became the focus of all consideration.

Being leaders in so many areas, in 1978, even before the state of California imposed smoking bans in public places, The Villages banned it during annual meetings. In 1990, San Louis Obispo became the first city in the world to ban smoking at all public places. It became a law in the State of California in 1998

By the end of 1979, 1,258 villas were occupied. The total population was 2,257 residents. The Villages now owned debt-free title to the golf courses and the hill lands. President Jimmy Carter was leading our country with Walter F. Mondale serving as his Vice President at the time.

After serving The Villages as General Manager since 1967, Robert Nelson resigned from his position in 1981. The Villages greeted a new General Manager, Jack Gordon in March of that same year; two months after the United States had a new President. Ronald Reagan assumed the highest office in the country. His Vice President was George H.W. Bush.

In 1981, keeping up with technology, the directors of The Villages Golf and Country Club approved the recommendation for the installation of its first computer. There were further studies done before the actual purchase of the system. That same year, IBM introduced its first PC (personal computer) which put computers in the home for the first time. This allowed people who were not necessarily technically trained the opportunity to stay current with technology. Apple computer had a personal computer in 1977, but it utilized a TV screen and the owner needed to know how to wire, program and set it up.

The Villages' computer system became a reality in August 1981, when a Digital Equipment Corporation (DEC) VAXft Model 410 computer was installed. It included two video display terminals, two point of sale registers, a printer and associated software. In August 1994, one of the point of sale systems was installed in the Terrace Room, portable bar, The Grille and the Pro shop.

In February 1997, a computer lab opened in Cribari Center which housed several personal computers. This lab served the residents as a classroom. As more and more residents became computer literate and they put computers in their homes, it enabled greater communication, not only between each other, but also between staff and the Boards of Directors.

Continuing Education

An active senior community is more than just physically, active bodies. It is well recognized that it is also important to keep the mind active. Starting in December 1984, a series of educational programs, in cooperation with the San José Community College Services Department were offered to the residents. Lectures and discussions supplemented with slide presentations were presented by the faculty. They were held in the Cribari Conference Room.

This philosophy was expanded in January 2002 with the formation of The Senior Academy for Education (SAFE). Its mission statement is: "To develop, promote, and support stimulating and provocative programs that contribute to the intellectual life of the members of the Villages Golf and Country Club and the surrounding community." This organization presents seminars, lectures, debates, discussions, workshops, et al, to stimulate and intellectually challenge participants in the Arts, Sciences, Social Sciences, Languages and Current Events. There has been active participation from San José State University (SJSU) and Evergreen College.

Besides the discussion groups with SAFE, there are two clubs that use a similar format. First is the Philsophy Club whose topics for their meetings are chosen by the members of the group. One of the members does the research and gives the presentation for the group discussion. There is also the Ethical Humanist Club that attracts individuals who wish to discuss theories of all sorts. They meet monthly and are led by a member who presents a topic or a video for discussion. The programs are chosen by the club leader or suggested by the group.

The Bernard Osher Lifelong Learning Institutes were founded in 1978. The classes offered are for senior adults and are located at over 100 colleges and universities from Maine to Alaska and Hawaii.

Here at The Villages, in 2005, an Osher Lifelong Learning Institute affiliated with San José State University (SJSU) was instituted. In this capacity many classes were offered at The Villages. When SJSU found it necessary to make major budget cuts in 2009, the Osher program at The Villages was cancelled. In 2010, it was reinstated with Santa Clara University as the host college.

Age restrictive communities were new when The Villages were organized in 1967. At that time a resident was required to be at least 45 years of age. In November 1983, there was a Supreme Court ruling overturning these restrictions. Legislative action was undertaken to relieve the impact of this decision on senior communities. A bill was presented that would set the minimum age at 45. In January 1984, the debate was still going on in the California Legislature. There were four bills sent to Governor Deukmejian's desk, each with a different age restriction; 45, 52, 55, 62 years. It was resolved at that time to set the minimum age at 45. In 1986 this was changed, setting the minimum age of at least one of the residents at 55 years. This became a federal law in 1988. Abiding by this new law, in 1988, The Villages mandated that one person who resides in a home must be 55 years of age or older.

In June 1986, Jack Gordon resigned his position as General Manager and was replaced by Edward (Ted) W. Throndson. Nationally, George H.W. Bush and Dan Quayle won the presidential election in November 1988.

Universal Development L.P. of Northern California, a California Corporation (UDC) became the developers of The Villages in December 1984. In August 1985, UDC acquired more land for the development of 1500 additional homes. The land was purchased from Guy F. Atkinson Associates of San Francisco. UDC, as a result of this purchase, was now the sole owner of all the undeveloped property at The Villages.

Across the ocean, another piece of history occurred in 1961, when The *Berlin Wall* was built in Germany. This separated East and West Berlin and prevented visitation of families and friends across that border. Though it did not affect

The Villages directly, many residents had family members in East Germany. Ronald Reagan made his famous speech in 1987 telling Mr. Gorbachev, "Tear down this wall." It was two years later, in November 1989 that the wall was removed and the East German government announced that the citizens could now freely cross back and forth.

There was a proposal before the San José City Council in October 1989 to make the winery, winery office and boiler house part of a Wehner Historical Landmark Site. After a protest of over 300 Villagers, the City Council voted to give the designation to the mansion and related buildings, but excluded the winery complex which was owned by UDC.

This spared the Villages over a million dollars in refurbishment costs and long-term maintenance expense. It also gave The Villages a great deal of freedom in how the winery buildings were utilized or ultimately demolished.

The main arguments stated that:
1. The impact on the financial life savings of the residents.
2. There would not be any public access to view what would have been preserved. Even the residents would have little opportunity to view it.
3. The buildings were not particularly historic or architecturally important.

A piece of history was about to disappear, when in August 1992, plans were made to demolish the winery, built in 1908 to allow for the construction of a new corporation yard. The corporation yard at that time was by the 7[h] hole of the golf course, where Village Highland is now located. The maintenance facilities at that time were composed of a scattering of trailers, makeshift sheds and old barns. The city threatened to shut the current structure down, if a new one was not built to replace it.

As a result, plans were put in place for a new corporation yard. The new yard would include a maintenance shop, equipment and chemical storage, extensive parking, fueling facilities, storage of bulk materials, as well as rooms for offices and restrooms. The new corporation yard was completed and officially opened in December 1994.

The old winery building was built in 1890 and by 1989 was preserved for storage use only. It housed maintenance equipment; activity related items, as well as the barreling of Mirassou wines. Then, when a need for more land for the construction of Villages Olivas became evident, the last remaining building from the original winery was torn down.

After a year of proposals and discussions, in 1991 a decision was made as to the use of what was known as The Strip (the area to the right of the Security Plaza as you leave The Villages). The plans called for a recreational area for the residents in a park-like setting. There would be cart paths, benches, shuffleboard and over 400 plants and trees. This proposal never came to fruition and the area has remained as a lovely grass area that is used for croquet and an occasional Bocce game.

After General Manager Ted Throndson left The Villages, Steve Glantz was hired as the new General Manager on December 23, 1993.

A growing community usually means changes and that was the case in 1990 when the business offices; General Manager, Assistants and Accounting moved from Cribari Center into Building A by the tennis courts. Building A was the former sales office for the developers.

Building A

The Community Activities Office relocated from Cribari Center (the present Senior Resource Center room) to Building B right next to the main staff offices in August 1997. Building B, C and D were the original models for the Village Montgomery villas. That same month, the decision was made by the Board of Directors to not allow any future commercial enterprises in Cribari Center.

Buildings B, C, D

The Community Resource Center in Building B became the location of the Villages' Copy Center in June 2002. It offers services, for a fee, that includes single black and white copies, colored paper, transparencies, labels, reductions, enlargements and stapling.

As a result, changes took place in Cribari Center. The VMA took over the manager's office including the outer office that had been occupied by Theresa Jepson and Diana Camagna, the General Manager's assistants. The former community activities office became the sewing room. The old accounting office was converted to general meeting rooms and the library expanded into the old board room.

In August, an *Ice Room*, located at Cribari Center, was opened for the use of the residents. Stocked in the room is bulk party and event ice. In addition, food refrigeration and freezer storage for scheduled organizational events is available. Residents, for a small fee can use the food storage for personal events.

The Villages embarked on a major construction project in 1995 when UDC presented the plans for a new clubhouse. With the approval of 1,192 Villagers voting to build the clubhouse, the groundbreaking was held October 2, 1995.

The Clubhouse had its grand opening in September 1996. It included a café for casual dining, a bar and a large room for group events and meetings. The large room was designed to be more flexible in its usage, by dividing it into three sections with sliding partitions. The three rooms were given individual names in order to identify them. The Fairway Room is the section that looks out across the golf course. The Sunset Room is on the west side of the facility and the center room is named the Oak Room. The floor in this section is oak, making it suitable for dancing.

The community's yearning for fresh vegetables and fruits was satisfied when in June 1998 a Farmers' Market set up their stalls in the Cribari Center parking lot. The first farmers market opened in Los Angeles, California 75 years ago. Over the years they began to spring up all over the country. Downtown San José saw its first farmers' market in 1992.

Geoff Smith became the new General Manager in August 1999 replacing Steve Glantz who had resigned in June.

The early part of December sees The Villages lighting up like a veritable fantasyland as residents decorate their homes and the clubhouses for the Holiday season. A festive mood prevails as friends and neighbors gather for holiday parties and celebrations. The Christian community erects a Nativity scene on the corner of Villages Parkway and Fairway Drive to depict their meaning of the season.

The Jewish community in celebration of Chanukah erects a Menorah, which was designed and built by Adam Cintz. It is also displayed on the corner of Villages Parkway and Fairway Drive. The candles on the Menorah are lit as the days in the Chanukah season are counted.

Evergreen Development

Over the years Evergreen and specifically the neighborhood of which The Villages is a part has expanded offering many services to The Villages' residents. Progress generally means changes.

The groundbreaking for Eastridge Center was October 1968 on the former Hillview Golf Course. The center opened in 1970 with over 150 stores, theaters and office buildings. It was the first enclosed mall on the West Coast.

An Albertsons Supermarket opened in Aborn Square; a shopping center on Capitol and Aborn Road, joining a pharmacy, a cleaner and some restaurants and shops that were already there.

In February 1971, there was a presentation in Cribari Auditorium by Dr. Otto Roemich, president of San José City College and superintendent of the San José Community College District. The subject was the proposal of the planned Evergreen Valley City College. May 1975 was the date of the first graduating class. The college is situated on the 155 acre site on Yerba Buena Road near the corner of San Felipe Road, adjacent to Montgomery Hill. After opening, Evergreen College Library dedicated a room to the history of the Evergreen area of San José, called the Heritage Room.

On March 22, 1976, the San José Public Library opened a branch in Evergreen on Aborn Road. 2006 saw the construction of a new library building on the same site.

San Felipe Road was expanded to four lanes from Yerba Buena Road to Aborn Road in 1977 and in 1978 a redesigned bridge on Yerba Buena Road was built.

In May of 1979 Guy F. Atkinson Associates sold the Parkway land (on the north side of Villages Parkway) to the Derk Hunter group (The Plaza Group). Construction for a shopping center on this parcel of land, to be named, The Villages Plaza, began in June 1979. The first phase included the Bank of America, a market, a barber shop, a video store, Allstate Insurance and a savings and loan institution. The beauty shop and pharmacy originally located in The Villages also moved to the new center. After the Bank of America vacated the building in The Villages and moved to its new location in The Villages Plaza in 1980, they donated the temporary building that they had been using to The Villages. It became known as The Club Room. Improvements to San Felipe Road also were made at this same time.

The Villages Plaza

In May 1982, Lake Cunningham Regional Park on White Road, east of Reid-Hillview Airport opened. It is an artificial lake for the enjoyment of the people in the San José area. An addition to the site a few years later was the Raging Waters Theme Park. It is the largest of its type in Northern California. Its proximity makes it a wonderful venue for visiting grandchildren.

In December 1988, Retirement Inns of America announced plans to build a facility on the northeast corner of San Felipe Road and Villages Parkway. Instead of this facility, in August 2001, construction began on the Villagio housing project on Villages Parkway. It was completed in 2003. There are three, two-story buildings in the complex with a total of 79 apartments.

Development of a new park, in 1991, called the Linear Park for Evergreen, located on Yerba Buena Road includes a jogging trail, basketball park and a grass area for other activities.

A new community center known as The Evergreen Community Center opened in Evergreen Park on the east side of San Felipe Road in January 1992. This center provides classes, as well as hot lunches at a reasonable cost.

An assisted living facility, The Regency, opened on San Felipe Road, north of Yerba Buena Road, across from the Cortese fruit barn in January 1995. The

Cortese fruit barn closed shortly thereafter. It had been a neighborhood land-mark for many years, selling produce such as freshly picked cherries in June to Christmas trees in December. A small shopping center was built in its place in 2001.

A second assisted living community named Sunbridge (now known as Vintage) was built on San Felipe Road in 1998.

Governing bodies of The Villages

Following is a description of the California Corporations, which were initially responsible for the management of The Villages. Since the founding of The Vil-lages Golf and Country club in 1967, some changes in the organization have taken place.

The Villages Management Corporation

The first corporation formed in 1967 was The Villages Management Corpora-tion (VMC). This Corporation was formed from the employees of Atkinson-Mackay. A general manager was assigned to direct the corporation. Their pur-pose was to oversee the other corporations by managing their affairs and keep-ing the records. This corporation was dissolved on June 30, 1983.

The Villages Golf and Country Club

The Board of Directors of The Villages Golf and Country Club, a Cali-fornia Mutual Non-benefit Corporation, is responsible for the management of club operations.
It owns the Cribari Center, including the craft rooms, the Terrace Room, and all the equipment. It owns all the other community centers as well, including the equipment, furnishings, the swimming pool facilities, the Pro Shop complex and the two golf courses. The club assumed all the responsibilities of the Man-agement Corporation when it was dissolved.

The Villages Association Corporation

The Board of Directors of The Villages Association, a California Non-profit Mutual Benefit Corporation, formed in 1967 and it is responsible for the management of the condominium areas. The condominium areas include the sidewalks, the villas, the landscape areas, the laundry rooms and the carports. The Villages Association is responsible for all the common areas associated with the villas, which include the exterior walls, the roofs, and the concrete floors. The Association carries the fire, liability, earthquake and flood insurance on all buildings within the condominium area. The interior of the buildings and the personal property is the individual owner's responsibility.

The Villages Homeowners Corporation

The Board of Directors of The Villages Homeowners Corporation formed in 1974 and is responsible for the management of the single detached homes. The owner of the home owns his lot and home and is responsible for the all maintenance inside and out.

The Villages Community Services Corporation

The Villages Community Services Corporation is a California non-profit corporation formed in 1967. The corporation owned and operated the CATV system, owned and maintained the streets, has responsibility for the maintenance of the utility system, operation of the Security program, the Service Department, The Weekly Villager and the operation of the motel rooms. This corporation was merged into the Villages Golf and Country Club on June 20, 1983.

Until 2003, the same group of directors served both The Villages Golf and Country Club and The Villages Association Corporation. At that time, two separate boards were formed each having seven members.

In 2000, the District Advisory Committees (DAC) were formed. Each village/district has a small committee of three to seven members who are appointed by the Association Board of Directors. The purpose of the DAC is to assist the Association Board by facilitating communication to and from the residents.

The Villages held an interfaith candlelight vigil of remembrance when for the first time in its history; the United States was attacked by terrorists.

There were a series of coordinated attacks by Al-Qaeda on September 11, 2001. Nineteen terrorists hijacked four commercial airliners and intentionally crashed two into the Twin Towers of The World Trade Center in New York City, killing everyone on board and thousands who were working in the buildings. The buildings collapsed in two hours, also destroying some nearby structures. A third airliner was crashed into the Pentagon in Arlington, Virginia, outside of Washington, D.C. The fourth plane crashed into a field near Shanksville, Pennsylvania. It was intended for Washington, D.C., but the flight crew and some passengers attempted to retake control, thereby never making it to Washington. There weren't any survivors from the flights. There were a total of 2,993 people who died in the attacks.

The horror of that morning will live in the minds of all Americans, forever.

Changes are constantly taking place as a community grows and society and technology continue to make huge strides. People find it necessary to constantly adapt to these changes. As a result, this chapter in the book will never be finished as we watch The Villages evolve along with new technology and social mores.

Aerial photo 2000 of The Villages Courtesy of Sandra Williamson GeoCadd

The Twelve Villages

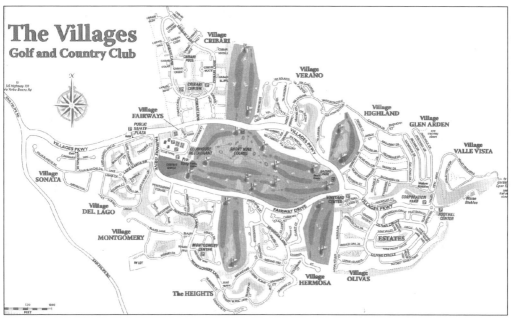

Courtesy of The Villages Golf and Country Club

The original concept of The Villages was to have seven separate Villages that made up the entire community. This gradually changed for a variety of reasons; for example, architectural differences or newly available property.

The final number of villages that now comprise The Villages Golf and Country Club became a total of 12. These 12 villages are: Village Cribari, Village Montgomery, The Heights, Village Hermosa, Village Verano, Village del Lago, Village Highland, Village Glen Arden, Village Olivas, Village Sonata, Village Fairways and Village Valle Vista.

The first village built by Atkinson-Mackay was Village Cribari which commenced in 1967. This village was aptly named Cribari after the family who owned and operated the winery on the property. The streets in Village Cribari all include the name Cribari. By June of 1968, there were 200 villas sold in Village Cribari. The architecture of these villas is in the California mission style.

A grand opening of the final section of Cribari, the Hillview Section occurred on May 25, 1969.

There was a specially landscaped knoll on Cribari Lane where an Olé Rose Garden was planted in honor of La Fiesta de Las Roses, the yearly festival which was held in San José. The Olé rose is San José's official flower and a symbol of the fiesta.

Before Cribari was completed, construction began on the second village - Village Montgomery. The models in Village Montgomery opened on March 15, 1971. Prospective buyers had requested some three-bedroom units and this was satisfied in the newly executed drawings of the floor plans for the new models. The prices ranged from $23,000.00 to $57,000.00. The average cost of a new house nationwide was $27,550. The villas in Montgomery were single storied homes with almost half having flat roofs.

This opening coincided with an event in Evergreen Valley honoring John Montgomery. His name was well known in the area due to his accomplishments in the field of aerodynamics and the decision was made to name the newest village after this historical figure. Construction of the roads began in June 1971 and the condominiums began shortly thereafter.

Though many of the streets in Montgomery were named after John Montgomery, there are some that hold names of other historical individuals. Wehner Way is named after William Wehner, the original owner of the winery. Gerdts Drive, Whaley Drive and Blauer Lane were all named for early settlers in the Evergreen area, particularly those associated with the property The Villages occupies.

The first section of Village Hermosa opened in August 1974. The word Hermosa in Spanish means beautiful; a very fitting name for this newest village. A brand new housing concept was introduced for this third village by Terra California, the new construction company. For the first time, townhouse living was brought to The Villages in a condominium style called haciendas. The white stucco walls, dark wood trim and tile roofs depicted early California Spanish style homes. Soaring vaulted ceilings accented the interiors of these two story buildings. There were five different floor plans offered and built by Terra California.

As the village grew, it also became the first village to include some single family homes. The first of these was built on Claret Court in 1977. The owners of those parcels of land contracted with their own architects for the design of their residences. Several of these homes were positioned to face out toward the fourteenth fairway of the golf course.

The streets in this village took on the names of numerous varieties of wines, considering the historical nature of the property.

Nestled between Village Montgomery and Village Hermosa is the village named The Heights. Again, names of wines were chosen for the street names.

This village was originally a section of Village Montgomery. Ultimately, The Heights became recognized as a separate village.

Proposition 13 was approved by the voters of California in June 1978, which slashed real estate taxes by 60 percent. It was wonderful for the senior community, as it also put limits on the percentage the county could increase taxes as long as you remained in the residence you were living in at the time. After the bill was passed, a person could make one move and keep the tax base. This protected senior citizens from being taxed at a rate so high that they could be forced from their homes.

Village Verano construction began in June 1979. The name Verano means summer in Spanish. One can only speculate why this was chosen, other than construction began in the summer. The first homes opened along the third fairway in October 1979. Village Verano is split by Villages Parkway. The homes on the north side of the parkway are known as Norte Verano and the homes on the south side are known as Sur Verano, but they exist as one village. Again, some individual homes were constructed in the Norte Verano area.

In 1982 the plans were on the drawing board for the next village to be built. The original name on the plans was Village Vaquero (translated means cattle tender). By the time construction began in the summer of 1985, the name changed to Village del Lago (translated means of the lake). It is located in close proximity to the entrance, across from the shopping center and adjacent to Village Montgomery. In the plans for this new village were many lakes; hence the name. This was United Development Corporation's (UDC) first construction project at The Villages. Many of the street names include lake.

Skipping ahcad 11 ycars, initial grading began in November 1996 for a new village: del Lago II. Construction by the current contractor, Shea Homes began on del Lago II in March 1997. By the time it was built, the name was changed to Village Sonata. A return to varieties of wines became the choice for naming the streets.

The final clearing of the old Mirassou Vineyards was concluded making way for Village Bodega; meaning warehouse. Again, a name change to Village Highland occurred by the time construction actually began in April of 1987. The reason for the change was that the homes did not look Spanish and reminded the builders more of Scotland. It was for this reason that the naming of the streets also took on the flavor of Scotland.

Construction of Village Glen Arden began on December 3, 1992. The original plans were for this group of homes to be part of Village Highland. The architecture was in contrast to Village Highland, so the decision was made to name it Village Glen Arden which is also Scottish in origin. The streets also have names that suggest a Scottish heritage.

In September 1990, the land was cleared for Village Olivas. This village was named for the row of Olive trees that lined the road to the Wehner mansion, which are evident along the section of Fairway Drive that travels along the north side of Village Olivas. This village was the first to have sidewalks. After a long delay, the city of San José granted the permits in January 1991 and the grading commenced. Construction began in August 1991 and the models opened in January 1992.

The street names in Village Olivas reverted back to the operation of the winery. Both American and French Oak were the woods used in the wine barrels. Lomas Azules was the name that William Wehner named his mansion. Solera is the old winemaking process whereby wine trickles down from one barrel to another. Ranch House, Fruit Barn and Garden House were all buildings connected to the Wehner, Haentze and Cribari estate and were vital to the operation of the winery.

January 1994 saw the demolition of the old winery barn to make way for the next section of Olivas.

In April 1995, 22 new homes were planned next to the tennis courts. Construction for Village Fairways began in November that same year. Its streets: Wimbledon and Clubhouse relate to the proximity to the tennis courts and the Villages Clubhouse.

There was some major dirt moving in November 1996. The dirt was removed from the old garden site where Village Hidalgo was going to be built. It was moved to the center of Olivas to build up an area for some individual homes, ultimately called The Estates, which would be part of Village Olivas.

Construction for Village Valle Vista (changed from the original designated name of Village Hidalgo) began in November 1997. The models were similar to those built in Village Olivas. The street names as well as the name of the village reflect the spectacular views from atop the hill. This village was built on a hill overlooking the rest of The Villages.

Over the span of 43 years, the exterior appearance of many of the villas and homes has changed somewhat due to color changes as the homes were re-painted.

This completed the construction of the community known as *The Villages*. There are 2,535 residences (2,309 villas and 226 individual homes), each one with its own characteristics. The diversity in architecture creates a beautiful individualistic community.

Photo taken from the Kuhn Ranch over looking The Villages

Set amidst rolling hills and surrounding the golf course; the setting is idealistic.

Clubs and Organizations

The curtain was going up for a stellar performance on Broadway; *Cat on a Hot Tin Roof*, a revival. The Tony Award for the best play in 1975 was *Equus*.

Three thousand miles west, the curtain went up in Cribari auditorium for the first performance by the Villages Amateur Theater Group (VAT). This was a performance of a short play *My Shadow* at the Halloween Ball in October 1974. The following spring, VAT performed its first full play, *A Night at Minsky's* (Minsky's was an east coast burlesque theater).

"Who Dunit" 1978

The Arts and Crafts organization originally sponsored VAT. In 1980, VAT formed their own club. They have continued to please sell-out audiences ever since.

In 1993 VAT expanded with the formation of a second performing arts group. The Readers Group (or Theater of Imagination) is a group that performs in a format reminiscent of drama programs on the radio. They do not use props and read directly from the scripts. Their first performance was *The Odd Couple*. Further expansion in 2010 was the addition of another group of performers called Readers Abroad. This group performs as an outreach to outside venues, such as convalescent homes.

Until the mid 1980's, there was a sewing room complete with sewing machines for the Villagers' use. Some women formed a group called Needles and Threads for those who loved to sew. One of their philanthropic endeavors was the support of Friends Outside, a group dedicated to helping families of those in prison. Beautiful knitted garments and cozy quilts were made and presented to the children to bring a little sunshine into their lives. Ultimately, due to lack of participation, the sewing room was shut down and the machines were sold.

Heard again was the whir of sewing machines in 1999, when The Villages' Quilters was formed. They started by meeting in people's homes and then in May 2000, the meetings moved to the Forum and eventually to the Patio Room. The quilters meet to share their projects, help and inspire each other. The

group continued to grow through the years. Evidence of their work is shown at the yearly art shows where the members' quilts are beautifully displayed for the enjoyment of the Villagers and their guests.

One of the amenities of The Villages is the popular and frequently used wood shop, which is equipped with a complete set of power tools. Having left their private woodshops at their former homes, new residents were delighted to see the equipment that was at their disposal. Training provided ensures that residents who use this facility are familiar with the safe operation of all the tools. The woodshop was available for use beginning in November 1968 and has been a very valuable asset to The Villages. The Villages has benefitted with the gifts of furniture, cabinets and more, which were crafted by the able woodworkers.

To witness some incredible creativity and talent of the Villagers is to visit a Villages' Arts and Crafts event, such as the first art show in 1975. One of the amenities that The Villages offered to early residents and that continued through the years was a full spectrum art studio, with separate rooms for pottery and lapidary. Classes offered made it possible for

anyone interested to try their hands at some form of craft.

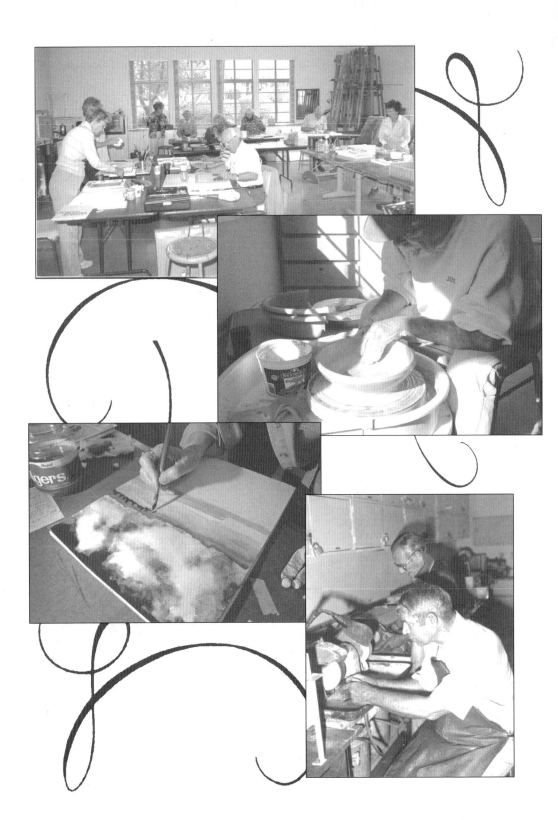

Beginning in 1972, the Arts and Crafts Association sponsored a *Holiday Faire* with handcrafted treasures for sale. Over the years, it grew in size and became a holiday tradition. The experience of shopping within The Villages, with music playing and friendly, helpful vendors, brings residents back; along with guests year after year. The Villagers and their guests are treated to a selection of gifts that are unique due to the creativity and dedication of the artisans.

The history of this event began when a few women in the ceramics room were making gifts for their families. A vision came to one of the women, "Wouldn't it be fun to sell some of our merchandise?"… and that was just the beginning.

Cribari auditorium became home to an event that featured painting, ceramics, lapidary, photographs and much more for the first Holiday Showcase Arts and Crafts Show. The show ran for two days in September 1972. Due to its success, within two years, the now Christmas Boutique became a major event with the Drama Club and the Choir participating by giving performances.

Calling on their creativity, the committee changed the theme, yearly with such names as, Christmas Country Faire, Calle de Tiendas (street of stores) and Mission Fiesta. The latter showed Cribari decorated to look like the front of a Mission, complete with mission bells. The craftspeople dressed like friars and señoras in colorful skirts. The event continued to grow to include a bake sale, drawings for prizes, piano music and a slide show.

In 1989, less than one month after the Loma Prieta earthquake, the sale moved out to the patio as some necessary repairs needed to be made in the auditorium. "The show must go on" was the attitude of the organizers. A large green and white tent was set up on the patio - fondly referred to as the Big Top. The decorating was adjusted and the results produced another successful event.

In 1991, theme creativity grew to Eiffel Tower heights, as the decorating committee created Vive les Arts. Flower carts and Parisian street lights turned the auditorium into a veritable Parisian scene. The bake sale became Vive Le Boulanger. Holiday shoppers were immersed in a shopping trip to a virtual Paris.

The annual event financially benefits both the craftspeople and the Arts and Crafts Association. Vendors pay a percentage of their sales to the Arts and Crafts Club. Wall hangings for the Conference Room, benches at Vineyard Center, golf course markers, stage drapes and lights are a few of the donations made possible as a result of this event. The artisans prepare their crafts all year and the rest of the residents mark their calendars in anticipation of this successful yearly Holiday Faire.

Gazebo Park was the venue of a second artisan show in September 2001; Art in the Park. Held in the spring, this beautiful setting provided another opportunity for the craftspeople to share their artwork. Shoppers could stroll among the tables laden with original creations while sipping wine and sampling food. An accordion and accompanists provide music.

Then in December 1996, the Villages Boutique became a reality, just in time for the holiday season. The Holiday Faire had demonstrated success and an idea for a year-round boutique was suggested. An available room in Cribari Center became this small boutique. It has been very successful over the years and eventually expanded into a second room. The Boutique serves Villagers with merchandise that is handcrafted by fellow residents.

An additional very creative group is the Camera Club. With monthly challenges and competition, they are continually growing in their expertise. Having professional judges who also critique their work for the competition is also instructional. This training for the photographers helps them improve their skills in composing what they see through the eye of the camera. All of the residents benefit by the rotating display of photographs at several sites in the community. The Camera Club has been instrumental in creating videos about The Villages.

Another room in Cribari Center became the Villages' Investment Resource Center (VIRC). The VIRC, for minimal dues, makes available an extensive library of investment newspapers, magazines and newsletters, which is maintained by a club of the same name. Once a month, VIRC sponsors professional speakers on the subject of finance and investments which is open to the community.

Popular in the fifties, were Booster Clubs. The Villages formed their own Booster Club in 1970. It was their responsibility to manage the growing number of activities at The Villages. This group was replaced by an Activities Committee in 1972 which was originally chosen by a resident vote. Their purpose was to plan, organize and run a variety of events for the residents and advise the Club's Activities Department on social, cultural and recreational activities at The Villages. The group disbanded about 2002 and the community activities came under the auspices of the Clubhouse Committee and the Activities Department.

A significant number of residents, when they moved to The Villages, had a second home on wheels or a boat. Shortly after construction began in The Villages, a temporary location was designated for storing recreational vehicles. This area was where Village Verano is located today.

After a long wait, in 1978 the trailer, recreational vehicle (RV) and boat storage moved from the Verano area to a permanent location at the far south-west corner of The Villages, next to Montgomery Village. The developer fenced the area and The Villages provided the utility service for the vehicles. An RV Club was formed and many club members travel together several times a year. Some of the excursions are close, such as the Monterey Jazz Festival while others take them to distant locations such as Mexico.

Maybe Old MacDonald was famous for his farm, but many Villagers have the same passion. They moved to The Villages from all over the country, many having had flower as well as vegetable gardens. A popular feature has always been the availability of garden plots. These plots give enjoyment to those residents who wish to turn the fertile earth and have it produce their own vegetables and or flowers. The green thumbers formed The Garden Club in January 1969 and in February 1970, the gardens became a reality. As a gift to The Villages, in January 1971, the Garden Club purchased some plants to beautify the parkway.

Initially located in the area where Village Verano now stands, the gardens have made several moves. Building of the residential homes forced the location of the gardens to slowly move up the hillside. In 1978, the gardens were moved to an area east of the 17th fairway and in 1986, they were on the move again due to UDC wanting more building sites. They were temporarily closed in November of that year anticipating a move to the hill lands.

Hopefully for the last time, the gardens moved again in 1995. The plans called for a total of 45 plots that would be located in the hills above the Villages. In 1998, a gazebo became an addition to the garden area.

There are approximately 65 clubs in The Villages. Widely varied in nature, there is literally something for everyone from flower arranging to artists' books. Other than those already mentioned in this chapter and other places in the book, the following gives a short synopsis of some additional clubs.

Two popular Villages' events are the yearly Vienna Café and the Oktoberfest, both sponsored by the German Club. Villagers gather for good food, lively polkas, Viennese waltzes, and an afternoon of *kameradschaft*.[1] The German Club meets monthly with varied dinner programs. Reminiscent of days gone by, they spon-sor a traditional carol sing at Christmas time.

Both the Italian Club and Club Latino meet to enjoy great ethnic food and fellowship. Each of these clubs sponsors special programs to be enjoyed by all Villagers.

Almost any day of the week, in the Ladies' and Men's Lounges and the Terrace Room, there will be various games in progress. Two very popular games are Dominoes and Mah Jongg. In addition to these are many card games of Pinochle and Bridge. Bridge games are also played in the Clubhouse accompanied by lunch.

Sons in Retirement (SIR) is a Northern California men's group. The Villages has two active branches. Their monthly luncheon meetings feature a variety of speakers. They also have inter-club golf tournaments and sponsor tours.

There are three separate clubs; (The Vermilion Villagers, The Scarlet Sirens, The Crimson Charmers) that wear red hats as their identifying symbol. These groups meet to just have fun, by lunching or participating in some event. At Christmastime, the three clubs join together to collect toys for children.

In order to keep The Villagers well-informed politically, there is both a Democratic and a Republican Club. These groups feature speakers who are can-

---

[1] camaraderie

didates for public office, or current men and women in the political arena who address issues of the day.

There are small dogs and large dogs, from Chihauuas to German Shepherds that live in the residences with their faithful owners. The Dog Lovers Club was formed in order for the dog owners, as well as their dogs, to meet with others that have similar interests.

Our local university, San José State University boasts many graduates who have chosen to live in The Villages. These graduates, as well as individuals who may have a relative or friend who is associated with the university, or people who are just interested in the university, formed a club named Friends of San José State. They have a dinner meeting at the Clubhouse once a year, to which they invite a speaker from the university's staff.

Philanthropic work is at the forefront with The Villages chapter of The Philanthropic Educational Organization (PEO). It is a nation-wide group that raises money by donating used clothing to a designated shop. The money raised is used to help financially, needy students attend college. The PEO has speakers geared toward subjects that will improve the mind.

We all gaze at stars, but the Amateur Astronomy Club is serious about it. They meet once a month to gaze as well as hear speakers from NASA, physicists and other astronomers. Trips to Fremont Peak to use their telescope, trips to see meteor showers and *starbeques* are all part of their activities. Fortunately for the group, some local colleges have observatories. The college observatories are open to the Villages' Astronomers.

The Villages Amateur Radio Club (VARC) was formed about 1983. Sometimes referred to as Ham Radio, the group in The Villages originally had their equipment in an old trailer and an antenna nearby. When the old cable TV shack became available in 2009, VARC relocated to that facility. They are an integral part of EPC and would be in full operation in the case of a disaster. Often, in the case of a disaster, such as the Loma Prieta earthquake and the hurricane, Katrina, government and commercial communications may be out of service. The ham radio groups make the all-important communication possible. They also maintain cooperation with the Santa Clara County Emergency Services.

With so many diversified clubs that are offered, the need for socialization and learning is satisfied. Some of the clubs have been established since the formation of The Villages and others have been formed as the various interests arise. One only has to imagine what will be offered in the future.

Volunteers of Time and Talent

What is a volunteer? According to *Random House Dictionary*, a volunteer is; "a person who voluntarily offers himself/ herself for a service or undertaking; a person who performs a service of his/her own free will."

That is only part of the description of an individual who offers their time and talent. The individual is led by his heart to be of service to the community.

The Villages is a unique community due to this feature. Much of why there are so many activities and beautiful pieces of furniture is due to the generous gifts of time and talent that the Villagers give for the benefit of their fellow residents. Just as they do today, the early residents of The Villages pulled together and shared their talents.

One of these was Hank Volle, an accomplished artist who lived in The Villages. In 1972, he used his talents to design the bell tower logo that graces everything  from letterhead paper to golf score cards, the original stickers on the windshields of the cars, golf jackets and sweaters. Hank was always interested in the bell tower at the corner of Villages Parkway and San Felipe Road. "…when I was asked to design a logo, I thought about doing something with the tower." "When things needed to get done, we (the residents) did them", Volle said. He volunteered his efforts and when UDC acquired the construction of the homes, the logo became the most recognizable symbol of The Villages. The logo has been registered with the State of California as a Service Mark.

The Club Board, the Association Board and the Homeowners Board are all formed with dedicated volunteers. Anybody who has served on a board of directors knows how many hours are given to the task. These men and women give back to the community that serves them so well. They take this responsibility very seriously and as a result help to maintain the lifestyle and ambiance of The Villages, as well as planning for future improvements.

Each of the boards has a Rules Committee. Its members review the current rules and evaluate them in accordance with the needs and safety of the residents as well as the changing times and laws.

The Architectural Control Committee was formed in February 1974. Their responsibility is to maintain the architectural continuity and aesthetic appearance of The Villages. When entering the gate and driving up Villages Parkway, one can see the care and planning that has gone into not only the homes, but the landscaping around the homes and in the common area.

There were changes made in 1975 to the makeup of the committee and it was placed under the jurisdiction of the Board of Directors. At that time, it was comprised of a resident as chairman, a registered architect, a representative from the Developer and a Villages' staff member with non-voting status. This individual served as secretary and processed the paperwork as well as keeping the records.

Over the years, three architectural committees evolved. One serves the needs of The Villages Club, one for the Association (the Villas) and one for the Homeowners (individual homes). The Villagers who serve on these committees give freely of their time to ensure that the beauty of The Villages is maintained and protected.

The Villages' Alliance was founded in 1980. Its purpose is "To promote friendship among residents and appreciation of The Villages and understanding of its plan of operations, as well as propose and support measures that will contribute to its success." The organization holds quarterly meetings at which there are informative speakers who address issues of interest to The Villages. They also host a Candidates' Night for the individuals seeking election to each of the three Boards of Directors.

The Villages has four swimming pools and to keep them running smoothly there is a Swimming Pool Committee. They address safety issues and the general operation of the pools.

Further benefits offered by the VMA occurred when funds were raised in 1992 and arrangements were made with the Visiting Nurse Association to have a part time nurse at The Villages. It soon became apparent that a social worker would better fill the needs of the residents. Information is professionally dispensed concerning rest homes, assisted living and other concerns of an ageing community. In 2005 the VMA donated automatic door openers for the café to better accommodate the handicapped.

The Convalescent Home Ministry is part of the VMA. Clothing such as: socks, lap blankets, shawls, scarves and hats donated by residents are gathered by this service organization. These items are often hand knitted or crocheted by residents. Other donations such as stuffed animals and Bingo prizes are also accepted. A member of the committee then delivers these items to hospitals and convalescent homes. At Christmastime, sweat-suits are purchased with donations from the VMA and delivered to grateful recipients.

Senior Resource Services (SRS), another part of the VMA was formed in 2002. SRS assists residents who seek information for future planning. The motto of this group is "Villagers Helping Villagers". Since its inception, SRS has grown from five volunteers to more than 15 volunteers. These individuals have varied backgrounds in accounting, law, insurance, investments, banking, antiques and collectibles. The staff answers routine questions, gives out appropriate literature and when necessary directs Villagers to paid professionals. They offer assistance, which is free and confidential, relating to the complexities of financial situations, as well as aiding in the location of care facilities and help of many sorts. In addition, general and timely information is communicated to residents at large by the SRS through *The Villager*.

Upon entering the café, you are greeted by hosts and hostesses. These gracious volunteers are residents of the community. When the new Clubhouse opened with its larger restaurant, this new service was initiated. The hosts and hostesses lead you to an available table and present you with a menu. They keep a watchful eye and are there to help with making your dining experience pleasurable.

The Clubhouse has its own committee that plans clubhouse events, such as dinners, fashion shows and teas for the community.

The High Twelve has contributed abundantly to The Villages. Each June, the proceeds from the Pancake Breakfast are used for their many donations to The Villages. They also placed special trash cans in the dumpster areas. Beginning in 1990, these containers were designated for the recycling of aluminum cans. Some of the profits from these two activities are used for the benefit of The Villages. Over the years, the High Twelve Organization has given many pieces of furniture, including a piano and the grandfather clock that proudly stands in the foyer of the Clubhouse Café. The lovely round picnic tables and benches at Gazebo Park, the benches outside the café and concrete benches along the walking paths are due to the generosity of the High Twelve Club. In 1991 High Twelve donated two 5,000 watt generators for use in emergencies. Some chairs for the Pool Room, the scoreboards at the Bocce courts and some bookcases for the VMA office are also gifts from the High Twelve.

The Men's (golf) Club donated the tee markers for the golf course in The Villages in 1980.

The golf course has a Bandini patrol. The name Bandini relates to fertilizer and other nutrients for growing plants. June of 1986 saw the formation of the Villages' Bandini patrol. This group of golfers meets at 8:00 a.m. every Monday morning and fills the divots, as well as helping to improve the tees in general.

The Evergreen Villages Foundation (EVF) was founded in 2009. "The mission of the Evergreen Villages Foundation is to solicit funds to support capital improvement projects that promote and maintain the physical , intellectual, social health and general well-being of the Villages community's 4,000 + active senior adult residents." The Foundation is a 501(c)3 nonprofit organization. All contributions are tax-deductable to the extent allowed by law.

The woodshop which is located in Cribari Center is the focus of a tremendous number of projects. Most times when you walk past the room, you hear the whirring of the table saws and smell the aroma of freshly cut wood. Don Yamada and the talented individuals in the woodshop made the mailboxes for various clubs that hang in Cribari Center. In 2002, they also donated the ballot boxes that are used for elections.

In 1975, a showcase was built and donated to The Villages by Clif Baxter. He put in over 80 hours of work in the woodshop and the end result was a beautiful cabinet. It stands in the Café lobby and serves to display residents' special collections.

It would be remiss not to mention those who donate their time to organize the popular 4th of July Parade and decorate The Villages for the Holiday season.

Breakfast with Santa is a fun event which occurs just before Christmas for the children of The Villages' employees. Donations for the gifts come from the various clubs and the event is orchestrated by volunteers.

A large bell was hung over the entrance to the Café shortly after it opened in August 1996. It was donated by three of the Villages' golf groups; the Swingers, the Men's Club and the Belles.

A beautiful feature also as you enter the Café is a fountain located between the entrance and the Pro Shop. This was donated by the Activities Committee. If you look into the water, you will see coins. A memory of "Three Coins in a Fountain" comes to mind with a promise, not to return to Rome as in the movie, but to the Café.

Besides these group efforts, many individuals have shared their talents and stepped forward with much appreciated donations, many of which are anonymous. The following is just one of these stories.

Historic Bell donated to The Villages

Another beautiful bell located at the entrance to the Cribari Center was donated by residents Bea and Clyde Snyder. The following story tells the history of the bell as written by Bea.

"As a youngster I loved spending summer vacations on my uncle's cattle ranch in Southwestern Oklahoma. The bell hung in a funny little cupola atop the one room schoolhouse. It was used to call the children to classes during the school term, but in the summer it was rung to announce special events. Its tones sent every woman in the area to the multiple-party telephones to get the news. It could signal a picnic, a square dance, a potluck supper, a birth, a death or an emergency. I usually rode with my uncle and he would send me, my horse galloping, back to the house to learn why the bell was rung. As a city child I thought this was a pretty neat communication system. When progress doomed the school house many years later, my aunt had the bell crated and sent to me in California as a memento. It holds wonderful memories.

Clyde and I thought it a good idea to give the bell to celebrate our country's 200th birthday and to express our joy in living at The Villages. Perhaps we can establish a Villages' tradition by ringing it every July 4th to announce our own special events."

July 1975

There are many reasons why people love living at The Villages. All of them could probably be described as a direct result of the generosity of Villagers. Many, many people give tirelessly of their time. All you have to do is look around and see how each of the residents benefits from these gifts of time and talent. This is just one of the things that makes this community such a special place to reside.

The Villager

The first newspaper was published over 400 years ago. A newspaper is a source of information about events around the world, as well as the local community.

Today, in order to be informed, many Villagers have the *San José Mercury News* delivered to their homes. Looking at some history of this newspaper, we find that 74 years after the city of San José was founded, its first newspaper was published called the *San José Weekly Visitor*. The year was 1851 and this newspaper was to become *The San José Mercury News*. To set this in the time frame of the historical account of The Villages, Antonio Chaboya was operating the Rancho Yerba Buena. By 1942, the name of the paper had become *The San José Mercury*. *The San José Mercury* purchased the *San José News,* which had been founded in 1883, and published the two newspapers. In 1983, the papers were merged into the *San José Mercury News* we know today.

The word Mercury is frequently used in a newspaper name after Mercury the Roman messenger of the god of commerce, known for his swiftness. In the case of the *San José Mercury* an added reason was the importance of the element mercury in the processing of gold ore during the California Gold Rush.

In The Villages, information is also dispensed to the residents in a special newspaper, *The Villager*, which is delivered to every home. The first issue of *The Weekly Villager* was published by the Villages Management Corporation in January 1968.

Vol. I, No. VII   JANUARY 1968

For the first year, *The Villager* actually was two publications. One was a glossy four-page edition that was primarily used for potential buyers of a residence in The Villages. It had news of tournaments, views of villa models for sale and news about The Villages in general. It was distributed to the residents, along with a weekly supplement, called *The Villages Bulletin*, which was letter size, created on a typewriter and reproduced on a ditto machine. It provided notices about community events, a medical column, a restaurant menu and bus schedules.

The first week in February 1968, *The Villages Bulletin* added a copy of the masthead that was a replica of the one on the glossy edition of *The Villager* and included a calendar of events for the month.

In September 1968, the entire look of the newspaper changed. A name change to *The Weekly Villager* and a sketch of Cribari Center, with the graceful fountains in the foreground, was the new masthead. The tabloid sized (approximately 11" x 17"), four page newspaper on white paper now included such things as photos of the models for a fashion show, a list of duplicate bridge winners, a report from the men's nine hole golf group and small filler type articles such as neighborhood barbeques. The second page was devoted to religious services and for the first time advertizing appeared on the back page. The ads were two inches square and were laid out in a grid format.

Vol. 1, No. 9   THE VILLAGES, EVERGREEN VALLEY, CALIF.   Thursday, October 31, 1968

There were regular, weekly features such as a *Behind the Headlines* column that covered world news stories and an "Et Cetera" Column with bits of social news. The paper was prepared by the general manager and typed at The Villages. It was then taken to Valley Press for layout and typesetting.

Two months later it returned to the four-page letter size document. This size soon proved to be inadequate and it was necessary to include inserts with the overflow information. As a result, it returned to tabloid size toward the end of the year. The first page of *The Villager*, from its inception, has had a special Holiday cover usually in color.

Vol. 1, No. 123   THE VILLAGES, EVERGREEN VALLEY, CALIFORNIA   THURSDAY, FEBRUARY 25, 1971

By 1970, more changes took place. *The Weekly Villager* was typed and assembled in house by a staff editor. The creativity of the editor led to a variety of headers on the paper. The header now said *The Weekly Villager* in different formats. There were also frequent bullet notices on the masthead.

Weekly was eliminated from the title and sports pages were added in 1977, printed on green paper and inserted into *The Villager*. Then, in 1980, a new column named *Pulse Letters*; a new forum for residents' comments about current Villages' issues. Eventually a committee was formed to review the Pulse Letters for propriety and compliance with Pulse Letter criteria.

A big change occurred in 1985, when the paper used for *The Villager* became newsprint and the size decreased again. This change saved The Villages about $200.00 a week.

The Villager found a new home when it moved from Cribari Center to the office building (Building B) near the tennis courts in November 1991.

Over the years, coverage of community activities increased along with the size of the newspaper. By 2009, the paper was generally 32 pages. It has served as an effective source of communication between management, the boards of directors, the activities office and various organizations and the residents. The advertizing section eventually expanded to include real estate ads, personal items for sale as well as ads for services.

As with most things, growth in the community has affected and enhanced *The Villager*. Feature articles submitted by residents skilled in creative writing and news of the many special events in the community have made the paper an interesting document to read weekly. Each editor has brought their creativity to the publication in photography, as well as writing.

Geology and Earthquakes

The Villages is located in the eastern foothills of San José. The foothills are part of the California Coast Ranges, more specifically the Diablo Mountain Range. A significant mountain in the range is Mount Hamilton, which is located in San José and can be seen from The Villages.

The Santa Clara Valley is between the Santa Cruz Mountains to the west and the Diablo Mountain Range to the east. The valley was created by the growth of the mountains as they were thrust out of the earth's crust due to active volcanism, as opposed to erosion.

Prune trees courtesy of Oregon State University Archives

The Diablo Range is a verdant green during the winter and spring when the rains are plentiful and they turn a golden brown when the area dries out in the summertime. Until about 1970, the valley was ablaze with color as the prune trees and apricot trees burst into blossom. This gradually changed as the new product in Santa Clara County became the computer chip.

The hills surrounding The Villages, as well as the property upon which The Villages was built, produced abundant grapes and fruit, which ultimately gave way to the urban sprawl.

The Villages ranges in elevation from 467 feet at the front entrance to 2100 feet at the peak of the hill lands. Breaking this down, Cribari Center is at 488 feet; the Clubhouse is at 505 feet; Vineyard Center is at 648 feet; Foothill Center is at 792 feet; the highest house, which is located in Valle Vista, is 953 feet and the Gardens are 1,040 feet. This variation in elevation is particularly noticeable as you observe the progression of blossoming trees from the lower elevation to the highest.

The area where The Villages is located is very susceptible to the possibility of earthquakes. Three major earthquake faults run near The Villages. The Calaveras Fault is the closest, but the San Andreas and Hayward Faults are close enough to cause significant damage as noted in one of the episodes mentioned below. The Division of Mines and Geology went on record in 1976 stating, The Evergreen Fault, which may be seismically active, passes slightly more than a half mile southwest of this development. The potential for future earthquakes along this fault is unknown".

On April 24, 1984, a major earthquake with a magnitude of 6.2 on the Richter scale rumbled through The Villages. The epicenter was near Mt. Hamilton, east of San José, on the Calaveras fault. Fortunately, the epicenter was on sparsely populated hills. The quake occurred at 1:15 p.m.

There was an immediate inspection of The Villages by Security and the Service Department. Miraculously, there were no serious injuries and property damage to the villas, homes and club properties was limited. However, some Villagers lost treasured personal property.

The most serious damage was to the Wehner mansion, where two brick chimneys toppled and a large window was broken. Serious damage also happened to the old Winery building, in the section of the building that housed the landscape department's equipment. Also damaged were the south wall and the support of the south side of the roof. A part of the building used by Villages' organizations to store their property was in danger of collapsing.

Cribari auditorium closed until a complete safety inspection could be conducted. A cursory inspection of the beams indicated some movement had taken place.

Five years later on October 17, 1989 at 5:04 p.m., another major earthquake shook The Villages. It registered 7.1 on the Richter scale. This earthquake oc-

162

curred during the third game of the World Series between the San Francisco Giants and the Oakland Athletics and was the first major earthquake in America broadcast on live, national television.

This quake was centered in the Forest of Nicene Marks State Park in Santa Cruz County along the San Andreas Fault. The name given was the Loma Prieta Earthquake; for the nearby Loma Prieta peak.

The Villages again sustained some damage as a result of this earthquake. Cribari auditorium, which was now twenty years old, was given a *red* (unsafe) rating by a structural engineer, Mr. Peoples. The red designation meant that the auditorium could collapse during a major aftershock. Major cracks developed in the

huge ceiling trusses and the ceiling boards moved. The Villages was without electricity for about four hours, but the water and plumbing were fine. The Villages Communications Club shifted into action to prepare for possible emergencies. They used a car battery to keep the station running.

All events scheduled for Cribari were cancelled or relocated. Mr. Peoples had a crew inspect the other facilities and they were fine. As an interim measure, a tent was erected on the patio outside of Cribari Center and some social events were held there. The Villages purchased the tent with plans to use it for future special events.

Geography and Climate of the Area

There are four creeks that run through The Villages' property. The creek along San Felipe Road is named Thompson Creek. On the north side of the property is Yerba Buena Creek. Running along the south side of the mansion from east to west is North Cribari Creek. It eventually goes underground near the golf course. Along the southern boundary is Cribari Creek South.

With San José being a semi-arid area, there is always a concern about the supply of water for area crops. Albert Cribari kept track of the rainfall during the years he was involved with the Cribari Vineyards. He discovered that the rainfall was on an eleven year cycle. The vineyards were totally dependent on the yearly rainfall, as there wasn't any irrigation at the time. During the wettest years, the vineyard produced five to seven tons of grapes per acre. During the driest years they produced only one to two tons per acre.

As far back as 1977, there was a concern about water conservation. The Santa Clara Water District reduced The Villages' water allowance by 25 percent. This resulted in conservation efforts on the families who resided here.

At the other end of the precipitation related spectrum, 1998 saw an El Niño year that affected

Cribari Vineyards

California with quite a few major winter storms. In February, one of these storms wreaked havoc in The Villages, uprooting many trees, particularly on the golf course.

In spite of these periodic extreme weather cycles, San José maintains an ideal climate. Seldom are there freezing conditions and though snow has been recorded, it doesn't hamper driving. There are occasional heat spells, but our natural air-conditioning (the fog) usually rolls in after about three days. One of the reasons that California has grown so in population is due to its great climate. The beautiful green hills and blossoming trees in the springtime give way to the bountiful fruits and vegetables in the summer and the bold colors in the fall. In one day you can visit the snow in the Sierras and the ocean beaches on the coast.

To sum it all up…it's a beautiful place to call home.

Snow February 2009 Courtesy of Richard Mach

Fauna and Flora

In 1967, when the construction of The Villages had just begun, the site was a distance away from what would be called the urban area of San José. At that time, the rolling hills of Evergreen were sparsely inhabited except for the variety of birds and animals that resided there. As construction of new homes in The Villages as well as neighboring developments increased, the animals did not have the same freedoms they once enjoyed.

In many cases, the animals adapted to the change in their environment and continued to thrive. The deer added hybrid roses to their diet, the foxes found sleeping on chaise lounges to be very satisfying and the turkeys avoided the Thanksgiving Day table.

Courtesy of Scott Hinrichs

There is a very large herd of black tailed deer at The Villages. The does roam around at all times of the day. They give birth to fawns in the spring; frequently under the deck of a Village home. Bucks, though characteristically reclusive, are also seen by themselves or with other bucks. The does stay with their fawns in a very tight family unit.

Gray foxes stealthily walk around the Villages' streets. Most times, they are alone, but occasionally have offspring by their side. The gray fox is omnivorous and eats mice, rats, grasshoppers, crickets, eggs, birds, as well as acorns, berries and apples.

Masked thieves rummage around The Villages in the early morning hours. The raccoons look like cute little pets, but can be very nasty animals. They raid the gardens and pet food dishes. Their water sources dry up during the fall, before the rains come; as a result, they come into residential areas searching for water.

Wild pigs, also known as feral boars, have existed in California since the late 1700's. The origin of the pigs can be traced to the Spanish settlers who imported them. In 1920, some European wild pigs escaped from a domesticated breeder in Monterey County. These two breeds have interbred, which has resulted in the type of pig that roams here today. Over the years, The Villages has been plagued with destruction from these animals, especially the lawns. Like the raccoons, they are frequently seen during the fall when they come searching for water.

Wild Boar courtesy of Lucie Cole

In November 2003, an installation of an electric fence around part of the perimeter of the Villages helped deter intrusion by the wild pigs. This was part of a comprehensive program to limit the damage. There are three wires attached low on the existing chain link fence, two of these wires carry an electric current when the system is energized. This is high voltage, very low amperage and short duration current. If touched it causes pain, but no physical harm to the animals that encounter it. Even small animals like squirrels do not suffer physical injury from the jolt. The electric fence operates during darkness and at times when intrusion of wild pigs on Villages property has been observed.

Seen in our hills, from time to time are large cats, commonly known as mountain lions (also known as a cougar, panther or puma depending upon the location). They are tawny colored with black-tipped ears and tail. Adult males can be more than eight feet long, from the nose to the tip of the tail. The tail can be as long as the body. Generally, mountain lions are calm, quiet and elusive. They reside in areas with plentiful prey (deer) and adequate cover.

Bobcats occasionally walk along the perimeter of The Villages' property. They are about twice the size of a house cat. These cats are distinguishable by their cut off or bobbed tail and points on the tips of their ears.

With their long ears and fast gait, jackrabbits are very identifiable on the golf course as well as on residential lawns. With scrutiny, you can see cottontails close to the shrubbery. We all know the story of Peter Rabbit and Mr. Mc Gregor's garden. To protect their crops, the farmers in the Villages have fenced in their gardens.

Jack rabbit courtesy of Scott Hinrichs

Rattlesnakes and an occasional tarantula are infrequent visitors. Fortunately, they both have predators. One day a resident witnessed a turkey with a captured rattlesnake under his talons.

On January 29, 1970, Warden Harris from California Fish and Game, along with Jim Ross, golf course superintendent and James San Sebastian, project manager for Atkinson MacKay, evaluated the lake on the golf course for possible fish planting. In February, Robert Nelson, community manager stated that much thought and planning goes into preserving the natural environment of The Villages. Along with this thinking, in April 1970 there were some bass planted in the lake on the 16th fairway with resident fishing available on Mondays. After a short time, this was discontinued.

A surprise for The Villages occurred in July 2001 when a resident noticed a huge catfish in one of the Hermosa Lakes. Landscape Manager, Juan Heredia retrieved the fish. No one knows how it got into the lake.

An addition to a del Lago pond and other ponds in The Villages, in September 2002 was some mosquito eating fish. They are small minnow sized fish. The hope was that these fish would be a deterrent to the spread of West Nile Virus that was a concern at that time.

There is a treasure trove of our feathered friends at The Villages. Approximately 150 different species of birds have been sighted locally. Some of these winged wonders reside here all year long. Others appear during their migratory travels or when food becomes scarce at their regular habitat.

Small ubiquitous birds that are frequent visitors to The Villages include the Chickadee, Titmouse, House Finch, Lesser Goldfinch, and the Oregon Junco.

Oregon Junco courtesy of Michael Kulakofsky

Crow courtesy of Michael Kulakofsky

The crows, robins and Mallard ducks represent the largest numbers of birds in any species that reside in The Villages.

Robin courtesy of Michael Kulakofsky

Mallard duck courtesy of Michael Kulakofsky

Mary Fullerton, our local bird watcher authority, has divided The Villages into six different areas or habitats. They are the oak woods, suburb, edge habitat, scrub, golf course, fields and ponds. This is important to know in order to understand why the same birds are not found in every area of The Villages. Birds will visit those areas that provide them with their basic needs; food and shelter.

Buffleheads courtesy of Michael Kulakofsky

Visiting any one of the ponds or lakes within The Villages will give you the opportunity to spot Mallards, which can be seen all year long; Buffleheads, which come in late October and leave by late April; little black Coots with their bright white beaks and the graceful White Egrets, both the snowy and white.

Egret courtesy of Michael Kulakofsky

Some white ducks began migrating to The Villages during the early years of its development. A decision was made in 1975 to relocate them to area farms in order to preserve the beautiful strain of Mallard ducks that were beginning to appear on the lakes.

Also seen by the lakes are the statuesque Canadian Geese. Unfortunately, they can also invade the golf course, much to the distress of the golfers, as they are very messy birds.

Canadian geese courtesy of Scott Hinrichs

Our California state bird, the quail, with thcir little black plume bobbing up and down, are seen scurrying along the ground often followed by a flock of darling chicks.

Other ground feeders frequently seen are the Gold Crested Spans, the California Towhee and the Spotted Towhee.

Quail courtesy of Michael Kulakofsky

Kite courtesy of Michael Kulakofsky

Raptors are exquisite birds often seen circling overhead. The hawks include the Red shouldered Hawk, which has a screeching call; the Red Tail Hawk, which is seen on the golf course; the Kite, which loves to nest in high trees (one for the female with her nest and one for the male to stand guard); the magnificent Golden Eagle and the Osprey.

Red shouldered hawk courtesy of Michael Kulakofsky

One only has to drive into The Villages on a beautiful spring day to witness the magnificent blossoming trees. For the residents who love to walk or play golf, they can't help but admire the variety and beautiful specimens of trees that were either natural to the land prior to The Villages or planted with thought and care by the landscape gardeners. The earliest spring blossoms are the ornamental pears and plums.

Standing on the golf course, with your back to the stone gate, a row of Olive trees stretches out in front of you. This was the original tree lined road that led to the mansion, named Olive Lane by the Cribari family. You can imagine the horse and buggy and then the early automobile following this road.

More Olive trees that are younger have been planted along Villages Parkway and Fairway Drive.

The Olive tree is not native to this area. The early ranchers introduced them. It is an evergreen tree native to the Mediterranean, Asia and Africa. The olive is of major agricultural importance as a source of olive oil. In The Villages, some companies as well as residents have harvested the olives in order to produce some olive oil.

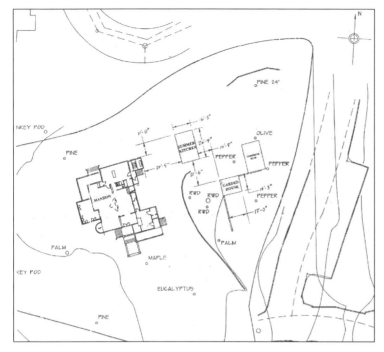

William Wehner took a great deal of pride in the landscaping of his estate. Some wonderful specimens of trees planted by him are still growing by the mansion. Four of these trees have been designated as Heritage Trees. (The San José City Council maintains a *Heritage Tree List* to provide official recognition and protection of trees on both private and public property that are of special significance to the community because of their history, girth, height, species or unique quality.) Two are Deodar Cedars; one is a Monkey Puzzle Tree and one an Italian Stone Pine.

Another tree introduced to this land by the early ranchers is the Eucalyptus tree. There are several on the golf course. Unfortunately, their root system is shallow and after heavy rains, resulting in soft soil, many of them have uprooted. Californians learned of this large, fast growing, evergreen tree from Australian miners. It grows easily in temperate climates and does not require much water. This wonder tree of nineteenth century California soon became known as America's largest weed. There was a eucalyptus boom in California about the same time that Antonio Chaboya received the patent for the Rancho Yerba Buena.

The Coast Live Oak trees, natural and prolific in the Evergreen area, are majestic trees with wide spreading branches. The city of Oakland was named after this particular tree.

There are two magnificent specimens of the Coast Live Oak tree within The Villages. The oldest specimen, estimated to be 275 years old and one of the largest trees in the valley, is found at the entrance to Village Hermosa (pictured above). The second in age is the one found on McCarty Ranch Drive, which is over 100 years old. A number of oak trees located on the site the Clubhouse now occupies were moved and transplanted in order to preserve them. The Coast Live Oak is distinguished from all the other oaks that are deciduous in the winter, while it is evergreen. In the latter half of the nineteenth century, the live oak was used for shipbuilding. Other oaks growing within The Villages are the Valley Oak, the Blue Oak, the Black Oak and the Scrub Oak.

Sweet smelling California Bay trees can be found growing along South Cribari creek, which is on the south-east side of The Villages. It is a native, evergreen tree. In the past, the leaf of the Bay was believed to cure headaches, toothaches and earaches. The Native Americans used the flesh and inner kernel of the fruit for food after drying them in the sun. Some birds find shelter in this tree as well as nourishment from the berries.

Today, the leaves are used in cooking. They are significantly stronger than the commercial Bay Laurel leaf. Some guitar makers use the Bay tree for their instruments since it has good tone qualities. Another name for the bay is Myrtlewood. You may find it interesting to know that bowls and spoons are often crafted from Myrtlewood.

Reaching for the sky is the stately, evergreen Italian Cypress tree, which grows abundantly throughout California. Their pyramid shape, which ends at a point at the top, is found desirable by many people. They can grow up to 80 feet in height. These trees are a rich, dark-green in color with very close knit foliage. The tree thrives in dry, sandy soil, which makes it very comfortable in California. It is not a shade tree, but very ornamental and is generally seen planted in a row of three to five. Many ornamental groupings grace different areas of The Villages.

The Chinese Elm is a tree that is evergreen when the winter is mild and deciduous when there is an unusually cold winter. The Chinese Elm spreads its branches to great lengths and they become weeping in nature as the tree matures. As a result, it is a wonderful specimen of a graceful shade tree.

The Coast Redwood tree has found a home in different locations in The Villages. This is the tallest tree in the world and can easily crowd out other trees. Generally, the tree only grows up to the fog line in the coastal mountains. However it does seem to do well in this environment as well. In their natural state, they arc usually found growing in clumps, but at The Villages, some beautiful specimens stand alone.

The Redwood tree has an interesting feature, the fairy ring (named by naturalists). Sprouts spontaneously erupt around the circumference of the tree trunk when it has been damaged or begins to die. Within a short period of time the sprouts develop their own root system and can grow to heights of eight feet during one growing season.

The ornamental tree, Liquidambar is recognizable by its five-pointed leaves and fruit that looks like a small ball with spikes. Sometimes called a Sweet Gum tree, it is deciduous and turns magnificent colors of red, yellow, dark purple and russet in the fall. Use of the sap is used for a base in salves, soaps and adhesives. In the southeast, it is a very important hardwood.

Another tree that bursts forth in color every fall is the Pistache tree. It is a deciduous tree that is actually native to China. Many beautiful Pistache trees can be seen along Villages Parkway. The fruit is visible as bunches of small red berries. (You will have to look at these trees in the fall to appreciate the vibrant color.)

The Willow tree, an example of which is by Montgomery Lake, is a deciduous tree that prefers moist soil. Willow wood is used to make boxes, toys and figurines. Flower arrangers love to use the curly willow branches in their creations.

The deciduous Sycamore tree can grow to about 100 feet in height. Its bark peals off leaving a mottled appearance. The fruit is ball shaped and falls from the tree in the winter.

A century plant blooms only once in its life. The Villages had one that graced the entrance in the late 1960's. The blooming spike grows very quickly, sapping all the strength out of the plant. The century plant was important to the indigenous people who used it for medicine, fiber, needles and food.

Cottonwood trees and the Big Leaf or Oregon Maple are scattered around The Villages.

For landscaping shrubs, The Villages is using more of the California natives, such as the Toyon and Coyote Ceanothus. These plants are drought resistant which saves on water usage as well as being mostly deer resistant.

The planting of ornamental cherry trees along the center strip of Cribari Lane in August 2000 enhanced the entrance to Village Cribari and the Cribari Center. In the spring the trees are amass with beautiful pink blossoms. A couple years later, in 2003, daffodils were planted amidst the trees.

The Villages had their own landscaping crew until March 2003. The board and ultimately the community saved more than $2 million over five-years after the landscaping was out-sourced.

Walking or driving around The Villages is like touring a botanical garden. We have such a variety of well-groomed trees and shrubs to enjoy. Step onto the golf course and see the beauty of the rolling greens and lush trees that dazzle the eyes. Add to this some personal touches in the small gardens around the residences to embellish the picture. Place a bird into the painting and you have a masterpiece.

Epilogue

We've journeyed through over 200 years of history. We began with the land that had natural grasses blowing in the wind to today's closely mowed and manicured grass. This is the panorama of time.

This land served to yield bountiful harvests and sights that are an artists and photographers Mecca. History was written here as distinctly as if it were carved on the walls of a cave or dug up by archeologists. Digging up this history at times was just as difficult. The deeper you dig, the more you discover.

History is never finished. What is current news today, becomes history tomorrow. It is affected by the changes in mores and lifestyles of the people who dwell on the land. We do not have a crystal ball that we can gaze into to see how this area will continue to transform, but we can be certain it will.

I only hope that you have been inspired to look more closely at this place we call home and appreciate all that has made it what it is today. We can be thankful for those before us who preserved the beauty and the history of the Evergreen area of San José and particularly The Villages.

Annette

Bibliography

Ancestry.com, Genealogy computer program

Arbuckle, Clyde, <u>Santa Clara Co. Ranchos</u> San Jose California 1968

City of San José   "The Urban Forest of San José",
        http://www.sanjoseca.gov/tree/trees_heritage.asp

Coe, Sada Sutcliff, <u>The Life That Was: The Story of Henry W. Coe State Park</u> 2009

Cribari, Eloise and Bob, <u>Cribari Family - interview with Anthony Cribari</u>

Douglas, Jack   San Jose History Museum article

Evergreen Times 31 October 1990

Evergreen Times August 1984

Evergreen Valley Echo March 1969

Garden of the World

Giordano, Loureen   "Winery Falls" <u>The Villager</u> June 16, 1994

Giordano, Loureen   <u>The Villager</u> 2 March 1995, 9 March 1995

Hall, Frederick   <u>History of San Jose and Surroundings</u>
        A.L. Bancroft & Co. 1871 p.284

Hiaring, Philip, <u>Wines and Vines Magazine</u> October 1991

http://www.wikipedia.org/ <u>Wikepedia Computer Encyclopedia</u>

Jepson, Theresa   <u>Villages Log</u> 1968

Leventhal, Alan,   <u>Back from Extinction</u>

Lockhart, Dr. Ben   <u>Personal Notes</u> 1968

Loomis, Patricia   "Signposts" <u>San Jose News</u>   September 14, 1979

Loomis, Patricia   "Signposts" <u>San Jose News</u>   March 10, 1978

Loomis, Patricia   "Signposts" <u>San Jose News</u>   August 20, 1976

Margolin, Malcolm, <u>The Ohlone Way</u> Heyday Books, Berkeley, CA 1978

<u>Mirassou Latest Press</u>   Vol. 4 1974

Newburn, Jewell,   "Early History" Written notes

Okrent, Daniel, "The Man Who Turned Off the Taps" <u>Smithsonian</u> May 2010

"Obituary" <u>Palo Alto Times</u>   Palo Alto, California February 20, 1928

"Obituary" <u>Palo Alto Times</u>   Palo Alto, California April 29, 1933

"Obituary Luisa Chaboya Long"   <u>San Jose Mercury</u> 1928

"Obituary Jeanie Chaboya" <u>San Jose Mercury</u> August 15, 1995 p.5B

"Outdoor California" <u>Department of Fish and Game</u> State of California
        November-December 1986

Rambo, Ralph   <u>Pioneer Blue Book of the Old Santa Clara Valley</u> 1973

San Jose Daily Mercury   San José, California   December 1, 1901 pp. 8-19
San Francisco Chronicle   June 2, 2005
San Jose History Museum Library
San Jose Mayfair December 3, 1964
San Jose News   March 14, 1940, February 25, 1961, January 26, 1966
"Out of the Past"   San Jose Mercury News
San Jose Mercury News   May 25, 1988
San Jose Mercury News   Evergreen Section 21 June 1989 p.3
San Jose Reporter Vol. 1 No. 80   June 17, 1959
Santa Clara County Hall of Records
Sawyers, Eugene T.   History of Santa Clara County
The Gold Post   June 1984
The Villager   The Villages San Jose, CA 1967 - 2010
United States Federal Census 1920, 1930
U.S. National Park Service reports
County of Santa Clara Death Certificate   "Wehner, William" # 28-011075
Wines and Vines Magazine   June 1937, October 1991

Personal interviews:

Vintner Families

Carmichael, Arthur (Son of Helen Cribari)
Cribari, Albert (Son of Angelo Cribari, grandson of Benjamin Cribari)
Cribari, Ted (Grandson of Fiore Cribari, great-grandson of Benjamin Cribari)
Frasse, Ebe (Daughter of Mary Cribari, granddaughter of Benjamin Cribari)
Mirassou, Daniel (Fifth generation of the Mirassou family)
Smith, Jerry (Great-grandson of Albert J. Haentze Sr.)
Tearse, Claire (Granddaughter of Thomas Cribari and Clementina Bisceglia)

The Villages:

Brand, Maria	Wehner History
Elderton, Chuck	Director of Maintenance Services at The Villages
Fullerton, Mary	Ornithologist, The Villages
Jepson, Theresa	First assistant to the General Manager of The Villages
Majerle-Tatum, Mary	Director of Community Activities at The Villages
Matei, Ileana	Director of Human Resources at The Villages
Meadows, Julia	Assistant to the General Manager of The Villages
Newburn, Jewell	Ohlone Research
San Sabastian, James	Project Manager Atkinson-MacKay

Leventhal, Alan, Archaeologist, San Jose State University   Ohlone Indians
Thompson, Peggy Kuhn   Rancho Yerba Buena formerly Kuhn Ranch
Verbica, Winnefred Coe   Rancho San Felipe formerly Coe Ranch

Essay in introduction to Chapter IX: Written by Jessie Levine, first prizewinner of
an essay contest sponsored by The Villages' Alliance in combination with the 20th
anniversary of The Villages. 1987